THE
LAND BANK
REVOLUTION

THE
LAND BANK
REVOLUTION

How Ohio's Communities Fought Back
Against the Foreclosure Crisis

Jim Rokakis and Gus Frangos

First Edition 2020
ISBN: 978-1-950-843-23-7

Parafine Press
3143 West 33rd Street, Cleveland, Ohio 44109
www.parafinepress.com
Cover design by Andrew Rokakis
Book design by Meredith Pangrace

Dedicated to Robin Thomas, teacher, friend, and mentor to Ohio land banks

Contents

PROLOGUE

Jim Rokakis

I met Mrs. Franklin (not her real name) at one of the dozens of meetings I attended as county treasurer to discuss the foreclosure epidemic in America and how it was impacting Cleveland neighborhoods. She lived in a suburb, but had grown up in the Mount Pleasant neighborhood of Cleveland, which was where her mother lived until she had passed away the year before.

"You know, Mr. Rokakis, we all took turns staying with our mother. She never spent a day in a nursing home. When she died we put the house up for sale and we were going to take that money, pay for her funeral, and divide the proceeds between the four kids. Maybe even take a family vacation."

The problem for the family was the fact that the foreclosure crisis had ravaged her old neighborhood and left hundreds of homes vacant. Many were vandalized and stripped of anything of value, just as her family home was eventually stripped of all the mechanicals and vandalized. The house was now worthless. She came to see me because she hoped the newly formed county land bank would take the property off of their hands.

"I am glad my mother didn't live to see this," she said.

The peak of America's foreclosure crisis is now more than ten years in the past. Students graduating college this year were just toddlers when the crisis began to ramp up in 2000. They were entering the fourth grade in the fall of 2008 when the lid blew off of America's financial markets and Lehman Brothers collapsed, Bear Stearns became insolvent and was sold to JP Morgan Chase, AIG was taken over by the Federal Reserve Bank, and Fannie Mae and Freddie Mac were put into conservatorship by the Federal Housing Finance Administration. Most importantly, that was the year when the Treasury Department was forced to bail out the American banking system with more than 700 billion dollars through the Troubled Asset Relief Program (TARP). These measures worked and the banking system has emerged intact—indeed, some would argue it is stronger than ever.

But for millions of Americans who lost their homes, the foreclosure crisis is not over. Their experience with homeownership has left them forever scarred. Homeowners in struggling cities like Cleveland, Dayton, Detroit, and Gary are still trying to recover from the mortgage meltdown and the Great Recession that followed. The equity that homeowners lost in 2007 and 2008 in Cleveland neighborhoods like Mount Pleasant and Glenville has never really returned. For these people the mortgage crisis is very much alive. Nothing demonstrates this better than this graph, which documents the collapse of housing values in ten Cleveland neighborhoods in 2007–2008, and how slow those values have been to return.

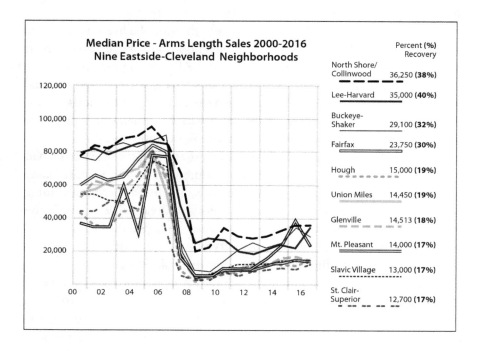

However, out of this crisis came a valuable tool: county land banks, powerful quasi-public corporations with extraordinary powers to take, hold, and repurpose vacant and abandoned properties. Started by then-Genesee County Treasurer (now Congressman) Dan Kildee, in Genesee County, Michigan, in 2004, this tool was brought to Ohio and improved upon by some sharp legal minds. In Ohio it became known as Senate Bill 353. When it passed out of the Ohio Legislature in December 2008 it was—and remains—the strongest land bank bill in America. A group of us in Cleveland, Ohio, led this charge—but the bill wasn't enough. We needed the resources to deal with the blight and abandonment. Over the past decade we have created the most powerful response to the foreclosure crisis in America. We have raised hundreds of millions of dollars at the federal, state, and county level, which has given us some of the funds that were needed to deal with wide-scale abandonment. But the money raised in Ohio through these various programs is not nearly enough to "solve" the problem of vacant and abandoned properties in this state. We are still billions of dollars short, as almost all of the money raised thus far has been limited to the removal of blight in residential areas. We have not addressed the thousands of closed and abandoned commercial and industrial buildings located in communities that once were thriving and made Ohio an industrial powerhouse—but are now vacant and serve as a constant reminder of a more prosperous past.

Western Reserve Land Conservancy has been directly involved in the establishment of more than fifty land banks in Ohio. Our staff has visited more than seventy counties in the state, and through these trips we have visited hundreds of cities, townships, and villages. Based on these travels I have often said that Ohio is, unfortunately, the "used to be" state. We "used to" make shoes here, we "used to" make cars here, we "used to" make steel here, etc. These perceptions are reinforced by the thousands of abandoned old factories, warehouses, and commercial buildings that remain empty—some now for as long as fifty years—that serve as a constant reminder of what we "used to" be, but prevent us from moving forward into what we can and should be.

This book examines how the foreclosure crisis came to Cleveland, and how as the Cuyahoga County treasurer from 1997–2010 I was in a unique position to witness the epidemic of foreclosures and the damage it caused to neighborhoods in Cleveland, Ohio, and ultimately to the entire county. It examines how we tried, and sometimes failed, to get the attention of policy makers at the federal and state level to deal with the crisis. And, most importantly, it explains how we fought back. We wrote and lobbied for the passage of a bill that allowed us to deal with the scourge of abandoned properties more quickly. We then wrote and passed a bill that allowed for the creation of county land banks in Ohio, but realized that a land bank without resources was, as the mayor of Youngstown once told me, like a "new car without gas." So we lobbied officials at the federal, state, and county level and raised hundreds of millions of dollars to deal with the crushing problem of blight and abandonment. The impact of these efforts has been tremendous and added billions of dollars back to Ohio's battered property tax duplicates, and restored some of the lost equity for homeowners in distressed communities.

Three of the chapters in this book have been authored by Gus Frangos, the attorney who serves as the CEO of the Cuyahoga County Land Reutilization Corporation, also known as the Cuyahoga Land Bank. Gus was a Cleveland city councilman from 1986 to 1993 and was particularly skillful at writing legislation. Gus wrote House Bill 294, the accelerated foreclosure bill we passed in 2006 when I served as the Cuyahoga County treasurer (Chapter Three) and Senate Bill 353—the bill that allowed for the establishment of county land banks in Ohio and integrated tax foreclosure and land banking (Chapter Five). He also explains the growth of the Cuyahoga Land Bank and the programs it has pioneered (Chapter Seven). His legal prowess was on display in both bills and because of their complexity nobody is better suited to describe the reasons why he wrote the bills, and how the bills worked, than Gus. It is no exaggeration to say that without Gus Frangos there would never have been a land bank bill—or county land banks—in Ohio. The people of Ohio owe him an enormous debt of gratitude.

Gus Frangos, Esq.

Nothing taught me more about urban affairs than serving as a Cleveland city councilman. I enjoyed being a councilman, mourned and rejoiced with constituents, made many friends, and passed many pieces of legislation. I came into office with stellar public servants like Dan Brady (now the county council president), Edward Rybka (a chief executive in Mayor Frank Jackson's cabinet) and of course, the visionary Hon. Raymond Pianka, who became the Cleveland Housing Court judge. He unfortunately is now deceased. They remained in government service. I went into private law practice in 1993.

In 2003, then-Cuyahoga County Treasurer Rokakis hired me to analyze and make suggestions for improving the tax foreclosure process. In the decades following my time in City Council, I often asked myself why my career took that turn. Though I believed it was a high calling, politics was not my life's ambition. Instead, I was going to raise my family, make plenty of money, and then go into the church mission field with my wife. But shortly after Jim hired me, the City Council thing started to come into perspective. Maybe it was providential after all. What resulted was a career that brought me back into public service in a way I never envisioned. I was able to deploy my skills for something much bigger than myself—the creation, implementation and operation of the Cuyahoga Land Bank. To Jim, many thanks for his trust in me and for giving me the opportunity to serve once again.

When I started working for Jim, he was seeing disturbing trends in the real estate market that very few people were acknowledging. He tasked me with analyzing whether the tax foreclosure process could be done more expeditiously, specifically with respect to vacant and abandoned properties.

Because many agencies touched on the tax foreclosure process, I needed to consult with key people with knowledge of the administrative processes. People like Michael Sweeney in the treasurer's office, James Bitterman and Shaundra Howard in the sheriff's office, Steve Bucha, foreclosure magistrate, Keith Hurley, deputy clerk of courts, and many others. These people embraced the need for reform as opposed to simply asserting "this is how we always have done it, no one is going to tell me what to do."

This process resulted in the 2006 passage of H.B. 294. The bill authorized administrative tax foreclosure of delinquent vacant and abandoned properties in the boards of revision (BOR). Once the bill passed, I became the coordinator of the BOR tax foreclosure docket in the Cuyahoga County Board of Revision.

Cases were expeditiously adjudicated through this tax foreclosure process. But by 2007 and 2008, in the midst of the financial crisis, tax foreclosure cases were flowing through the BOR process like a firehose. In 2008, Jim decided we needed to manage the ensuing chaos by creating a responsible repository that could accept and triage these properties as opposed to exposing them to speculative sheriff and forfeiture sales.

That led to the crafting of S.B. 353, which was signed into law in 2009. Nationally, it is considered the gold standard of land bank legislation. You will read the history leading up to the passage of H.B. 294 and S.B. 353 in Chapters Three and Five. You will read about the actual tools and techniques enabled by these two major legislative reforms. Finally, in Chapter Seven we will share the Cuyahoga Land Bank's results in the ten years following the passage of S.B. 353.

Chapter One:
The Coming Cataclysm

"I got houses being flipped and sold like nothing I have ever seen. . . .
This is flipping on steroids!"
—*Cleveland City Councilman Mike Polensek, August, 2000*

Jim Rokakis

It was August 2000. I had been serving as the Cuyahoga County treasurer for a little over three years. County treasurers are best known for sending out property tax bills, collecting taxes, chasing tax delinquencies, and investing the public's money. I was elected to office in November 1996 on the heels of a scandal—my predecessor had created an investment fund that, while legal, had run into serious problems and had to be liquidated at the cost to county taxpayers of $114 million. It was a disaster without parallel in the United States in the area of local public finance. There was a larger collapse in Orange County, California, but much of that money was recovered through litigation. This was not the case in Cuyahoga County.

I pushed the envelope as county treasurer. I wanted the position to be more than just the issuer of property tax bills and the collector of those funds. Early in my tenure I pushed to pass a state law that allowed for the sale of property tax liens. The tax lien sale brought in tens of millions of dollars that had been perceived as uncollectible. In my second year as treasurer, in 1999, I created a linked deposit program that made low-interest loans available to county residents who wanted to make home improvements to their residence. This low-interest home loan linked deposit program was issuing nearly a million dollars in linked deposit loans each month. This program, the Housing Enhancement Loan Program (HELP), is still available today. Since its inception in 1999, the HELP program helped to underwrite over 150 million dollars in home improvement loans in Cuyahoga County. Both programs were extremely successful. I was enjoying the job, but my world was about to change. I would spend the next ten years fighting fires that would grow to biblical proportions.

One day in August 2000 I received a series of calls from members of the Cleveland City Council, on which I had served for nineteen years. The most memorable of those calls was from Mike Polensek, the council member representing the Collinwood neighborhood in northeast Cleveland. Mike and I both came to the City Council twenty-two years earlier in 1978. He still serves at the time of this writing, making him the longest-serving council member ever. He was agitated, practically shouting at me, when we spoke.

"Jimmy, what the hell is going on out here?" he asked. "I got houses being flipped and sold here like nothing I have ever seen. I've got people buying and selling, and houses going vacant as soon as they are sold. It's killing the neighborhood!"

I suspected he was talking about the "flipping" of houses—a practice that isn't necessarily illegal on paper, but in practice often is. What makes flipping illegitimate, and often illegal, is when a party buys a property and makes cosmetic changes to that property only to sell it quickly, usually for an inflated price. These schemes often involve phony buyers, false appraisals, and sometimes even an insider at a financial institution that approves the suspect loan. He assured me this was worse. "I wish this was a guy just flipping a house or two. This is flipping on steroids!"

Later that same day, I also received a call from Housing Court Judge Ray Pianka, who had his hand on the pulse of the housing market in Cleveland better than anyone else. Ray was a highly regarded public servant, having served previously on City Council representing the west side neighborhood of Detroit-Shoreway, and having helped found the Detroit-Shoreway Community Development Corporation. Ray was widely regarded as the most knowledgeable person in Cleveland on housing matters. He knew Cleveland's neighborhoods better than anyone in the city and would often astound me with his knowledge of every Cleveland neighborhood— indeed, his knowledge of every Cleveland street, and often the history of individual homes. He was making the same observations and asking the same questions as Polensek. The calls troubled me, because they challenged me to speak out on something that I knew very little about: skyrocketing mortgage foreclosures that were occurring throughout the city and state. We weren't talking about property tax foreclosures, which I followed, but mortgage foreclosures being brought by lending institutions where property owners had stopped making payments. I had no idea what they were talking about.

I went over to see Judge Pianka that afternoon. He laid out a series of revelations for me that left me dumbfounded. Basically, he told me that the traditional lending model that I assumed was still in place, the lending model depicted by George Bailey and the movie *It's a Wonderful Life*, was dead. I knew and understood that model. When I bought my first home in 1980, I walked into the offices of the Broadview Savings and Loan Company and sat down with a banker who knew me. He approved my mortgage for $19,000 for a home at 3407-09 Archwood Avenue after I provided a 20 percent down payment and proof of employment. The judge talked to me about the old model—and how it was dying. He told me that it was being replaced by a new system involving mortgage brokers and the securitization of loans, and told me about how loans were going bad in Cleveland almost as quickly as they were being made. He pointed me to a couple of local professors at Cleveland-Marshall College of Law who could speak with great authority on this new lending model. One was Kathleen Engel, and the other was Patty McCoy. Both professors had been studying and writing about subprime loans (higher interest rate loans made to individuals with weaker credit) and securitization (a system that enables mortgages to be initiated locally and then packaged and sold to Wall Street, even loans of questionable quality). I had a lot of homework to do.

I immersed myself in the law professors' research and spent considerable time with them, particularly with Kathleen Engel. If George Bailey and that model of lending was dead, who was making these loans? Clearly something had replaced that old model as mortgages were flying off the shelves, and even more troubling was that foreclosures were following closely behind.

A bit of history is in order here. Home ownership rates in this country hovered between 40 percent and 45 percent until the end of World War II. Between the end of the war and 1965, the homeownership rate jumped to 64 percent, largely a result of returning GIs, Veteran's Administration loans, and a strong economy. That 64 percent number held steady until the mid-1990s, when the number began to creep up until it reached 69 percent in 2005. That 5 percent increase meant another 12 million Americans had achieved the goal of home ownership.

How did this happen?

Until the mid-1990s, the majority of mortgages in this country went to middle and working-class buyers with good credit. These mortgages were typically thirty-year mortgages at a lower, fixed rate. These mortgages required down payments of at least 10 percent, but often 20 percent. Subprime mortgages, mortgages to people with less than perfect or good credit, were rare and made up a small percentage of the market. These loans, like my loan at Broadview Savings and Loan, were held locally, effectively tying up this money for the length of the mortgage.

Beginning in the late 1970s, bankers at Salomon Brothers pioneered a new way of financing mortgages that involved the bundling of mortgages and selling them as bonds. The idea worked, as investors loved the returns and the safety of the investment. The low rate of home loan defaults and foreclosures led investors to reason, "What could be safer than American home mortgages?"

However, armed with calculations provided by financial wizards that demonstrated to investors that subprime mortgages could be bundled safely as well, bankers moved into the subprime mortgage market. The loans were a trickle that became a flood—and ultimately a tsunami. In fact, according to data provided by the Home Mortgage Disclosure Act, subprime mortgage loans increased sixteenfold, from 16,000 to 263,000 mortgages between 1993 and 1999. In 1995, subprime loans made up 5 percent of residential loans in the country, at $35 billion. Yet just nine years later in 2004, subprime lending reached a record $608 billion— nearly 22 percent of the residential loan market. As subprime mortgages took off, we began to see practices that would lead to the collapse of these markets. What happened to the traditional lending model?

Well, George Bailey was replaced by tens of thousands of mortgage brokers around the country who ignored their fiduciary duty to the borrower and instead placed millions of people into loans they could not afford. The brokers' compensation was commission based, and brokers were rewarded with higher commissions for loans that were good for the bank in that they charged a higher rate of interest— but not so good for the borrowers. These higher commissions were called "yield spread premiums," and included loans known as 2/28s or 3/27s—adjustable rate mortgages (ARMs) that kept introductory rates low for the first two or three years, but then adjusted upwards, usually with much higher payments. These were also referred to as "Exploding ARMs," because they blew up on the borrowers and often drove them into default.

But that was just one of the tricks used by brokers. With the full cooperation of the banks that underwrote these loans, they began to write loans that required no down payments, and amazingly, even had cash at the close for the borrower to use as they wished—although the stated reason was to make additional improvements to the property. (I remember meeting a property owner at a meeting in the Lee-Harvard neighborhood of Cleveland who told me he had six properties in foreclosure. He admitted to me that he had purchased the homes with no money down and had received thousands of dollars back at each of the closings to make improvements on the property, which I doubt he ever followed through on. I asked him what he did for a living and he told me "real estate investor!") Appraisers all over the country were working directly with buyers and sellers to determine how the appraiser could inflate the property value. Fraudulent applications to banks were filled with false information. In the industry, they were mockingly referred to as "Liar's loans," or NINJA loans: "no income, no job, no assets."

I must point out that there were "good guys" out there, like Third Federal Savings and Loan in Cleveland (the closest thing I ever saw to the Bailey Savings and Loan Company), but they were being replaced by an army of new lenders all over the country. Many of them were non-depository banks that were subject to very few federal regulations and little scrutiny. As these loans went bad, many of these operations shut down. I would follow their demise on a website called the "Implode-O-Meter." This website would keep a running track of the demise of these unscrupulous operators. Almost 400 of these lenders made it to the "Implode-O-Meter" by the end of the decade.

In short, I learned that the mortgage world had become the Wild West of lending and that Cleveland was the epicenter. What was happening in Cleveland—and the rest of Ohio—was spreading throughout the entire country, and the economic reverberations would be felt around the world. Noted author Alex Kotlowitz came to Cleveland to do a cover story on the real estate apocalypse for the *New York Times*. He spent days with Tony Brancatelli, the councilman representing the Slavic Village neighborhood. Slavic Village, ZIP code 44105, was the center of the mortgage foreclosure crisis—not just in Cleveland, but nationally.

When I began to look at these factors in the fall of 2000, the mortgage foreclosure rate in Cleveland was already the highest in the country. The average bank foreclosure rate in Ohio was twice what it was in 1995.

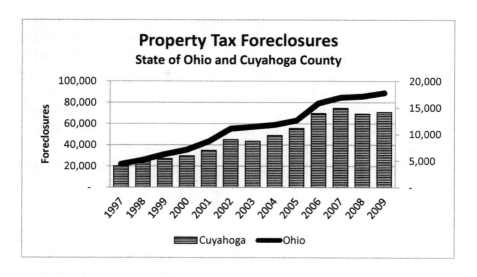

There were others in Cleveland who paid close attention to mortgage foreclosure data; one of those people was Frank Ford, an attorney and housing activist who worked for an organization called Cleveland Neighborhood Progress. Since 1995, he headed the Vacant and Abandoned Property Action Council (VAPAC). VAPAC was formed to deal with the scourge of vacant and abandoned properties in Cleveland, as well as the growing problem in the inner-ring suburbs. The organization's members were representatives of local and county government, legal and housing advocates, academics and members of neighborhood organizations. They came together under Frank's leadership because they believed the problem to be so serious that it required organization and collective action. The group met monthly to discuss the problem and potential solutions, including stronger housing inspections, more demolition dollars and legislative reforms that would empower local communities to deal with blight.

"Our goal with VAPAC was to bring together every agency that touched the problem of foreclosure and property abandonment; we couldn't combat the problem with each agency working in their own silo—we needed an engine that was firing on all cylinders," says Ford.

The Federal Reserve Bank ("the Fed") of Cleveland also attended many of these VAPAC meetings. The Federal Reserve Bank of Cleveland is one of twelve Federal Reserve Bank regional offices in the country. While the power of regional offices is limited, they have been helpful with research and have served as the convener of local and regional meetings. It was in this role that I asked Ruth Clevenger, the vice president and community affairs officer of the Cleveland Fed office, to serve as the convener of a meeting on the lending crisis. That meeting, entitled "Predatory Lending in Ohio," was held on March 23, 2001.

In preparing for this meeting, we scoured reports from the Fed, as well as public statements from Fed governors, to see if any of these comments might lead us to a keynote speaker to address the looming housing crisis. We learned that only one Fed governor—Ed Gramlich, of the Philadelphia Fed—was publicly critical of the increase in subprime mortgages. Howard Katz, a Harvard-trained lawyer and law professor who had taken time off from teaching to lead our research efforts, had studied Gramlich's speeches and writings. Katz requested, on behalf of the treasurer's office, that Gramlich give the keynote address for our conference. He agreed.

Our all-day conference featured speakers who focused on the foreclosure crisis, the Home Mortgage Disclosure Act (HMDA), the Home Ownership and Equity Protection Act (HOEPA), consumer protection, and other related topics. Gramlich did the same. He was measured and guarded in his keynote address and in his private comments to us, both before and after the address. Perhaps some of this guardedness resulted from the fact that then, the enormity of the crisis had not yet developed in Cuyahoga County, or in the rest of America. He wasn't so circumspect in 2007 when he published his book, *Subprime Mortgages: America's Latest Boom and Bust*. Though he was scholarly in his comments, his words were especially harsh towards the lending industry, blaming them for the crisis the country was facing. Sadly, he died of leukemia at age sixty-eight, a few months after the publication of the book.

The conference was well attended. There were almost 250 people there. I thought we finally got the attention of the Fed and believed that we would be traveling to Washington to meet with Federal Reserve Chairman Alan Greenspan or his staff. In retrospect, I was naïve. Our communications with the Fed from that point forward were friendly and sympathetic. They made it clear that our concerns had been passed on to the Fed both through the Cleveland office and through Ed Gramlich himself, but that there were no future meetings planned with anyone in Washington.

This was a huge disappointment. We really wanted an audience with Greenspan. Why? Because he was the most powerful central banker of our generation, and perhaps of all time. Economists believed that because of his stature, when he spoke, everyone listened. The skepticism he expressed in his 1996 speech about tech stocks and the tech market, coining the phrase "irrational exuberance" about the run up in tech stocks prices, is often cited as the reason tech stocks came back down to earth. We were convinced that all Alan Greenspan needed to say in one of his many speeches was that there was an "irrational exuberance" in the housing market, that loans were going bad as quickly as they were being made, and that these kinds of subprime mortgages were not good nor sustainable. We knew that the Federal Reserve Bank set monetary policy, but the Fed also played a critical role in directing regulatory policy for the nation's banks. If Greenspan had asked Congress to look at additional regulations for subprime mortgages and the loosely regulated non-depository banks, they would have listened. He could have shut down this dangerous mortgage game early—before so much of the damage was done. But Greenspan was enamored with the housing industry and, his critics would argue, simply replaced the technology bubble with the housing bubble. In fact, in a speech he gave in 2004, Greenspan was espousing the virtues of adjustable-rate mortgages!

We were in trouble—and it was about to get a whole lot worse.

Chapter Two:
The Contagion Spreads

"This is not just a city problem. It's a suburban problem, too.
It's an everywhere problem."
—*Georgine Welo, mayor of South Euclid, Ohio, May 2005*

Jim Rokakis

Our failure to get the attention of the Federal Reserve Bank after our conference did not bode well for our work. Foreclosures in Cuyahoga County went from 5,900 in 2000 to almost 7,000 in 2001, and the mortgage foreclosure rate continued to soar around the rest of Ohio as well. Ohio's foreclosure rate was triple the national average by 2005. That year, 1.4 percent of all Ohio households were in foreclosure.

Cleveland City Council President Frank Jackson had been working with housing activists on the possibility of enacting a local ordinance that could minimize runaway lending. Actions were simultaneously being considered in Toledo and Dayton as their foreclosure rates also soared. They realized there was very little help coming from the Fed, Congress, or from the Ohio legislature. They concluded that they would have to do it on their own through local ordinances. So, towards that end, all three communities passed anti-predatory lending legislation—Dayton was first in 2001, and Cleveland and Toledo followed in 2002.

The banking community in Ohio took notice of the Dayton ordinance, and lobbied the legislature in February 2002 for the passage of House Bill (H.B.) No. 386, which incorporated much of the 1994 Federal Home Ownership and Equity Protection Act (HOEPA). The bill also added new sections to the Revised Code (at R.C. 1349.25 to 1349.37 and R.C. 1.63) that addressed predatory lending in Ohio. Like the Toledo ordinance, HOEPA and H.B. No. 386 used various disclosure requirements and prohibitions to protect the public against high-cost mortgage loans. However, HOEPA and H.B. 386 set certain thresholds below which the statutes do not apply, and as a result, left most mortgages unregulated by state law. In general, HOEPA was viewed as a weak federal statute, and the foreclosure crisis still raged despite its passage. These weak consumer protection laws at both the state and federal levels, which left people unprotected from lower value subprime mortgage lending, were beneficial to the institutions making these loans.

Due to preemption, which is the authority of state and federal law to overrule the legislation of municipalities, H.B. 386 gave the banking community the legal grounds needed to challenge all three ordinances. They first challenged the Dayton ordinance, and lower courts ruled in 2004 that the Dayton ordinance was preempted by state law. Then the banker's trade association—the American Financial Services Association—challenged the other two ordinances. They filed actions in Cleveland and Toledo seeking declaratory and injunctive relief that their ordinances conflicted with state statutes. The Ohio Supreme Court was the ultimate arbiter in these cases, and by 2006, all three cases were decided in favor of the banks.

With the failure of local regulatory measures, and the continued inaction at all other levels of government, foreclosures continued their steady rise upward. In 2003, we experienced nearly 8,700 foreclosures in Cuyahoga County. In 2004, the number climbed to over 9,700. Much of the increase could be attributed to a new player who was wreaking havoc in Cuyahoga County, and particularly in Cleveland. That company was Argent Mortgage.

Argent Mortgage, along with its better-known sister company Ameriquest Mortgage, was owned by Roland Arnall. Arnall was President George H. Bush's largest contributor, and was also President Bush's pick to become ambassador to the Netherlands. Both Argent and Ameriquest Mortgage were housed under a holding company called Ameriquest Capital Corporation (ACC). The major difference between the two companies was that Ameriquest was an actual subprime lender, while Argent was nothing more than a wholesale lender using thousands of independent loan brokers all over America to originate and place loans with actual lenders. Ameriquest was under attack across the country for its lending practices and ultimately agreed in 2005 to pay states over $300 million to settle claims against it. In May 2006, Ameriquest announced it was closing 229 retail branches and laid off 3,800 employees. But Argent, unrestricted by Ameriquest's legal settlement, kept lending. So while Arnall had shut down Ameriquest, he knew Argent Mortgage had already taken its place

As treasurer, I was stunned by the growth of Argent. The name was everywhere. It seemed like Argent was making almost every loan in Cleveland. Well before Ameriquest was targeted by regulators, Argent was doing boom business in Cuyahoga County. In a county with over 600,000 parcels, they made over 45,000 loans between 2002 and 2004. Our county had never seen anything like it. Argent would soon become the largest subprime lender in America.

The filing of tens of thousands of mortgage and property tax foreclosures was clogging the Cuyahoga County Common Pleas Court system—not just with foreclosures on properties within the city limits of Cleveland, but on suburban properties as well. The increase in foreclosure filings in the inner-ring suburbs had skyrocketed. Suburban mayors concluded that they could not ignore this problem; it was their problem, too.

It had reached crisis stage, and no one knew this better than South Euclid Mayor Georgine Welo. South Euclid, a comfortable suburb of well-maintained homes east of Cleveland, had virtually no vacant homes in 2002. By 2005, the city had more than 200 vacant properties. Neighbors were calling her and demanding action.

"This is not just a city problem," I remember Mayor Welo telling me. "This is a suburban problem, too. This is an everywhere problem." It made sense. The people in the lending industry realized that they could make these questionable loans in suburban communities too, and because the sales prices were often higher these mortgages could be even more profitable for them. (I remember the irony of this as I met a man from Glenville who had sold his home there and moved to a suburban home in Richmond Heights, only to lose that home to a mortgage he could not afford. When I met him at a community meeting he had moved into his mother's basement—in Glenville.) The abandonment that Mayor Welo and so many others were seeing was caused by the simple act of a foreclosure filing. When homeowners received that notice of the foreclosure filing, many of them simply abandoned the property. They were struggling financially and didn't have money for an attorney—so they left. But they were still the legal owners. The bank didn't have the legal authority to enter the structure as they didn't hold the title. So these abandoned properties would begin to run down. The grass would go uncut. In some cases, the property was vandalized and stripped of its mechanicals.

On May 10, 2005, a meeting was convened at the Cuyahoga County Commissioners' Chambers in the County Administration Building. Mayor Welo and an organization made up of inner-ring suburban communities, the First Suburbs Consortium, largely drove this meeting. Invitations went out to suburban elected officials, along with the Cleveland community, including City Council and neighborhood housing advocates. All county officers were there, including the commissioners, the treasurer (me), the recorder, the prosecutor, the auditor, the sheriff, and the clerks of courts. The meeting was scheduled for 10:30 a.m., but by 10:00 a.m. the fourth floor commissioners' chambers were filled to the point of overflow and people were standing in the hallway. The high attendance was a testament to the severity of the crisis.

Testimony that day concerned vacant properties, their impact on the surrounding communities, the inefficiency of foreclosure proceedings in the court system, and the need for county assistance in dealing with the crisis. By the end of the meeting, county officials were convinced that we needed to break up the congestion of foreclosures in the Court of Common Pleas.

One of the results of the meeting was a program we created in the county treasury—the Cuyahoga County Foreclosure Prevention Program. This came about when lawyer and community activist Mark Wiseman pleaded with us to not only expedite mortgage foreclosures, but also offer foreclosure prevention assistance to the thousands who were facing foreclosure and were unable to afford a lawyer. Within six months of that meeting, with help from the Cleveland Foundation, Cleveland's largest and most influential foundation, the Cuyahoga County Foreclosure Prevention program was established with Mark Wiseman as its first director.

Our foreclosure backlog was complicated. The majority of the foreclosures being filed in Cuyahoga County courts were mortgage foreclosures, however there were significant number of property tax foreclosures in the system as well. Mortgage foreclosures are inherently more complicated because they often involve opposing attorneys, the filing of motions and multiple hearings. In the best of times, when foreclosure filings are not out of control, they could take upwards of two to three years to adjudicate. It was taking much longer because of the crisis— at least twice as long. Fortunately, in the case of at least some of the mortgage foreclosure filings, the properties often remained occupied and maintained. (Indeed, when I counseled people who were facing foreclosure I suggested they stay in the property for as long as they could—not just to use the time to save money for their inevitable move out, but to maintain and protect the property.) However, in the vast majority of property tax foreclosure cases, the properties were not only tax delinquent but also abandoned, and had been that way for a much longer period of time. These properties were damaging the surrounding communities. They were lowering property values. They were certainly affecting the confidence of the community. We had to find a way to take control of these vacant and abandoned properties more quickly.

It was clear to us that to break the backlog of foreclosures in the court system we would need to hire additional magistrates, and meet with the court administrator and chief administrative judge to express to them the urgency of moving mortgage foreclosures. As a result of that May 2010 meeting, all of those things happened. We hired additional magistrates. We actually paid for one of these magistrates out of the budget in the treasurer's office. The court developed a sense of urgency and we met regularly with the judges in the court to express the need to move these property tax foreclosures. But it was clear that we still had to find a way to separate these more damaging property tax foreclosures out of the traditional flow of foreclosure filings entirely.

Towards this end, I met with a former colleague from Cleveland City Council, Gus Frangos, who had just finished working as a magistrate in the Cleveland Municipal Court system and had transitioned to working as a private real estate attorney, and asked for his help.

Gus was a brilliant attorney who understood the complexities of foreclosure law from a civil litigation standpoint. In his first year of law school, he was first in his class and graduated with honors. He also understood Cleveland's neighborhoods and how fragile many of them were. He had some ideas about how we might be able to separate property tax foreclosures from the larger glut of bank mortgage foreclosures and expedite those of vacant and abandoned properties through a system of administrative foreclosure. As a former Cleveland City Council member representing a distressed Cleveland neighborhood, he understood how deleterious abandoned homes could be for a community. We hired him part-time at the county treasurer's office to write a bill that would break the log jam of tax foreclosures in the Court of Common Pleas—a bill that encompassed extraordinary and novel foreclosure reforms and came to be known as House Bill 294. Nobody can explain the process of writing the bill and its passage better than Gus Frangos.

Chapter Three:
House Bill 294

"Jim was seeing the impending financial crisis as clear-eyed as ever, but policymakers were not taking it seriously."
—Gus Frangos, Cuyahoga Land Bank President, 2019

Gus Frangos

I was elected to Cleveland City Council in 1985, re-elected in 1989 and retired in my last year—1993—to support my family of four and develop my law practice. Serving as a city councilman is like no other experience. I learned things about urban living, urban affairs, and municipal government that I would never have learned in a lifetime had I not served. It was a privilege, but for many reasons I needed to go back to my first love, practicing law. I had cut my teeth at the elite law firm of Ulmer and Berne from 1982 to 1985 and served on City Council from 1986 to 1993. I was appointed as a Cleveland Municipal Court Magistrate in 1993 by then administrative judge Larry Jones, who had served as a Cleveland city councilman with me. I served as a magistrate until 1997.

In 1998, I went into full-time practice as a litigation and transactional attorney gradually focusing on real estate, business transactions, and estates. In the spring of 2003 I had a chance meeting with County Treasurer Rokakis at a political event. I had served with Jim in Cleveland City Council. He began talking about negative trends he was seeing in the real estate market from the lens of the treasurer's office. He explained how community development groups were looking to him for solutions to tax foreclosure and housing destabilization. I thought to myself, "Why are you telling me all this?" As we talked, he explained some of the efforts he had been pursuing in lending practices reforms (at the level of the Ohio General Assembly, the Federal Reserve, and at the federal level). It was too much to digest at a chance social gathering, but that is how Jim rolled—always having the public interest in mind and a sense of urgency. In hindsight of course, he was seeing the impending financial crisis as clear-eyed as ever, but policymakers were not taking it seriously.

There was a limit, of course, to what Jim could do on the neighborhood level as a county treasurer. But that didn't stop Jim. A short time later, Jim asked me if I would be willing to work at the treasurer's office to analyze where there were inefficiencies in the tax foreclosure process and to recommend some changes. I agreed. Jim explained how tax foreclosure could be a useful tool for cleaning clouded titles of vacant and abandoned properties for redevelopment, but that tax foreclosure was a heavily bureaucratic and lengthy process. That process itself was impeding cities and community development corporations from acquiring and repurposing these vacant and abandoned properties. Only efficient and effective tax foreclosure could accomplish this by revising the standard tax foreclosure procedures, he explained. This would in turn help get properties back into responsible ownership and, of course, raise the tax base.

Things started slowly. Administrative officers and managers are often suspicious of an outsider, a "new kid" on the block, telling them how things ought to be done. Thankfully, Jim was well-respected throughout the county administration building and was viewed as a trusted and competent elected official. He quickly opened all the doors to all these offices, which was essential if I was going to propose changes. I learned to listen more and talk less at first. I spent approximately ten months researching and interviewing key staff members in the offices of the auditor, treasurer, prosecutor, clerk of courts, and sheriff to learn the internal administrative details of tax foreclosure practice at virtually every level—from high level tax collection policy to the day-to-day work of the office clerk who typed deeds and did data entry. This was a necessary process if we were to develop effective internal changes, let alone external policy reforms at the General Assembly level. Moreover, this also was important because it allowed me to establish relationships and to promote trust. You can have the best recommendations in the world, but if there is no trust, there will be no "buy-in."

With the help of these inside practitioners and a very skilled attorney in the private sector, Jim Sassano, who worked with the private foreclosure law firm of Carlisle, McNellie, Rini, Kramer & Ulrich, I was able to make select recommendations that would cut the time of a foreclosure significantly, in some cases by over a year. I was introduced to Jim Sassano when South Euclid Mayor Georgine Welo came to the county offices with an army of mayors and city managers demanding a more responsive and expedited tax foreclosure system (as discussed in Chapter Two).

I explained to Treasurer Rokakis that we could reduce the length of the tax foreclosure process by making small alterations in some of the administrative functions in the clerk of courts and sheriff's offices following issuance of the tax foreclosure decree. There was much duplication of effort, which was unnecessarily adding nearly a year to the foreclosure process. Several adjustments were suggested, many of which were adopted. However, it became clear that structural change was needed to truly expedite tax foreclosures, particularly of vacant and abandoned properties.

The first step was to better understand the problem we were trying to solve from an on the ground standpoint. Cleveland had a very mature network of community development corporations. They were adept at housing renovation and development, but they were impeded with legal and title-related issues that prevented them from quickly and efficiently taking control of tax-delinquent abandoned properties. These community development corporations might identify a property suitable for renovation at the time of a tax foreclosure case filing, but by the time the property was finally foreclosed upon and a sheriff's deed issued (sometimes up to four years later), the property had become vandalized and decayed to the point it was no longer suitable for renovation. The flow of these properties before the foreclosure cataclysm was very slow to be sure, but when properties became abandoned by the thousands and a turbulent real estate market took hold, tax foreclosure became extremely bottlenecked. Something drastic needed to be done to try to respond to the chaos and fix the problem on a structural level.

One structural problem was that tax foreclosed properties auctioned at sheriff's sale often involved tax delinquencies and assessments exceeding the fair market value of the property. In other words, the tax delinquency was so great that no one could afford to purchase these properties at the sheriff's sale let alone sensibly invest in them. Secondly, traditional tax foreclosures were taking between two and five years to complete. While some of this delay could be attributed to a lack of resources in prosecution and staff at the prosecutor's office, a lack of urgency, or the lack of priority given to tax foreclosures by the court system, the Rules of Civil Procedure themselves were a structural impediment to expeditious tax foreclosure, especially pertaining to vacant and abandoned properties. The Rules of Civil Procedure govern the procedures to be followed in civil cases generally in the county court system.

Procedurally, tax foreclosures were treated as any other civil case, such as a personal injury case, a contract, or business dispute. First, you had to file a complaint with the court. The Rules of Civil Procedure would then kick in; then came the (often deliberate) extension of time to answer the complaint; then came the answer itself; then there are two, three, or four case status calls; then the pre-trial conferences; then discovery, motion practice, and finally the scheduling of a default or summary judgment motion, or trial. All this for something that involved two basic questions: is there a tax delinquency and was it paid? In other words, there was an exorbitant amount of delay inherently built into the system to answer these two basic questions. I felt it was wasteful and inefficient.

Community advocates nevertheless were looking to Jim to speed up the tax foreclosure process for abandoned and decaying properties. Unfortunately, the county treasurer can only refer the delinquencies to the prosecutor for case preparation and filing, and even the prosecutor has no ultimate authority to accelerate the foreclosure actions. This was a function of the court's case schedule and docket management. And hence, it could take years for a case to be prepared, filed, and disposed of according to the system above. Jim asked me to begin by doing a complete top-down internal evaluation of the current system to see if it could be sped up.

In evaluating these internal processes, I quickly came to learn that tax foreclosure requires interaction between six separate governmental bodies, each of them separately elected by the public.

I had already been working on this issue when South Euclid Mayor Georgine Welo initiated the meeting with Cuyahoga County Commissioners Tim Hagan, Jimmy Dimora, and Peter Lawson Jones. That meeting was a powerful political punch to the solar plexus of county government and energized the process of addressing the tax foreclosure problem. Of course, it ultimately led to the writing a bill addressing the deficiencies in the tax foreclosure process as relates to vacant and abandoned properties.

The six county offices involved in tax foreclosure cases (and their respective roles) include: (1) the auditor, who first certifies the tax delinquency; (2) the treasurer, who attempts collection on these delinquencies through advertising and direct contact with the taxpayer; (3) the prosecutor, who prepares and files the tax foreclosure case if the treasurer is unable to collect; (4) the clerk of courts, who receives the complaint, dockets the case, and serves notice upon all defendants in the case; (5) the judge, to whom the case is assigned and who adjudicates the case and who then returns it to the clerk of courts with orders to the (6) sheriff—the sixth elected official in this process—to sell the property at sheriff's sale. Once the sheriff's sale is concluded, the foreclosure case is returned to the clerk of courts to docket the sale, then back to the judge notifying the judge of the sale results, who then confirms the sale. "Confirmation" is a term of art which means the judge signs off on the "regularity" of the sale of the property by the sheriff. Once confirmed, and the price and costs of the sale are collected, the sheriff finally issues a deed to the purchaser.

This was an admittedly complicated process and was made more difficult by the growing number of private foreclosures that were being filed by financial institutions. Even if one could control for internal bureaucratic inefficiencies, the process would still take two or three years, often more. What were some of the more glaring internal inefficiencies? Once the adjudication of foreclosure was decreed, under the old system, it could take weeks to send the order from the court (the judge) to the clerk of courts to journalize the decree and enter it onto the clerk's docket. Once the clerk docketed the decree, it had to prepare an "order of sale" to the sheriff to sell the property. The order of sale contained the legal description of the property and a recitation of the case information and decree. It would often take the clerk's office six months to prepare a property legal description and issue the order to the sheriff to sell the property. This was all by way of what is called a "praecipe" book, which chronologically logged every incoming decree of foreclosure one by one—tax foreclosure and private foreclosure. Once this order of sale was received by the sheriff, due to the backlog of cases, it would take several more months to advertise and schedule the property for a sheriff's sale. Once a sheriff's sale occurred and a buyer successfully bid on the property, the sheriff would again need to prepare a sheriff's deed. This again required the sheriff's office to manually type up a legal description yet again for the sheriff's deed. This manual preparation of deed descriptions by these offices independent of one another, added another four to eight months to the process, leaving the buyer of that property in a legal limbo long after they had paid for the property at the sheriff's sale!

I recommended some simple changes to this process. At the beginning of a tax foreclosure, a title report called a "preliminary judicial report" must be prepared by a title company which includes a "Schedule A," which is the legal description of the property. I recommended that instead of typing up the legal description manually multiple times throughout the process, that the decree provide the Schedule A description by way of an exhibit attachment; that same exhibit should be copied from the judicial decree and attached as an exhibit to the clerk's order of sale; and that same description should be copied and attached as an exhibit to the sheriff's deed. This simple recommendation alone sped up the process by months.

Cases would also get delayed for unavoidable reasons such as bankruptcy stays, *lis pendens*, or if a party to the case could not be found. If a defendant who had abandoned the property could not be found the service of process upon that individual defendant would have to be made by legal publication for at least three or four weeks in a publication of daily circulation, such as the *Daily Legal News*. I made a few other minor recommendations to these processes that sped the process up a bit. However, it became clear that legislative reforms were needed.

While researching potential reforms, I came across examples where tax foreclosures and tax enforcement occurred, at least initially, at an administrative level. Though many examples from other states didn't completely clear titles, there was no reason why the cleansing of titles using traditional Ohio foreclosure practice couldn't be embedded into our tax foreclosure system at an administrative level. Would an administrative agency or board be a suitable forum to hear and adjudicate tax foreclosures? Administrative tax foreclosures would eliminate the application of the Rules of Civil Procedure the same as virtually all administrative proceedings in the hundreds of boards and commissions at the local, county, and state level.

When considering this questions, I considered the role of the Rules of Civil Procedure, which guide the conduct of any civil lawsuit. These rules are designed to promote fairness, discourage surprises, flush out evidentiary issues, and establish timelines for the discovery of evidence and pre-trial motions in civil cases. We need these rules in civil cases because of the multiple legal and evidentiary issues that may arise. But in tax foreclosure cases, this is typically not the case. As a *statutory* proceeding under Chapters 5721 and 323 of the Ohio Revised Code, the issues are limited by the tax foreclosure statutes themselves to: (1) whether the taxes are delinquent; (2) whether the taxes have been paid; and, (3) whether all parties with an interest in the property can be served notice of the lawsuit. Clearly, unlike typical civil proceedings, there is typically no need to conduct extensive discovery and multiple unnecessary status conferences to determine whether a taxpayer has paid its real estate taxes. Yet tax foreclosures are subjected to all these same pre-trial practices and Rules of Civil Procedure as in personal injury cases, contract disputes, or divorce proceedings.

Because tax foreclosures are prescribed by tax foreclosure statutes enacted by the General Assembly, tax foreclosure is obviously a creature of statute. As such, I theorized that if the legislature created a statutory system of tax foreclosure as it did under existing law, the legislature could also create an alternative statutory scheme that was administrative in nature. In my research, I found other examples where states had adopted quasi-judicial and non-judicial foreclosure. I searched for cases that would speak to the constitutionality of administrative tax foreclosures. I found no impediments to the use of an administrative body adjudicating cases so long as there was access to the courts through appeal or other judicial oversight. Instead, the seminal cases dealing with foreclosure did not focus on the *forum* where the case was heard, but rather whether a property owner and any subordinate lien holders received proper notice and an opportunity to be heard in the proceeding, regardless of the forum. Believing there was no foundational constitutional impediment to administrative tax foreclosures, the method of achieving adequate notice to all owners and lien holders was simple. I would simply incorporate into the new statute the notice procedures contained in Civil Rule 4 of the Ohio Rules of Civil Procedure applicable to all lawsuits generally. This service of process under Civil Rule 4 would be perfected by the clerk of courts the same way as any typical judicially filed case. The difference however would be that an administrative case filed with the clerk of courts would instead be routed to the new administrative body rather than a judge. Civil Rule 4 and its counterpart in the Federal Rules of Civil Procedure have been universally deemed to meet the constitutional requisites of "notice and opportunity to be heard" by both the Ohio Supreme Court and U.S. Supreme Court. So although the Rules of Civil Procedure would not apply to administrative tax foreclosures, there were, in fact, useful and well-established precepts in a few of these rules which needed to be implanted onto the new statute to simplify the crafting of the legislation. Civil Rule 4 was one of them. Our deputy clerk of courts Keith Hurley was a godsend because he was willing to create a new numbering system for these cases and to docket these cases the same as any other civil case filed with clerk of courts, except with the prefix of "BR" (meaning board of revision) rather than "CV" (meaning a civil case). Without the cooperation of the clerk of courts, H.B. 294 would not have been possible.

Creating a tax foreclosure process through an administrative body necessarily meant that I had to identify the governmental entity or forum in each county that could hear these cases. One option was to simply create a new body within the county, and then identify qualified individuals to hear these cases administratively. I quickly dismissed this option. It would have required an entirely new chapter of the Ohio Revised Code containing the duties, qualifications, appointment authorities and method of appointment, guidelines, and more for the members of this new body. This would have been a heavy lift from a drafting standpoint, but happily it was simply unnecessary. I decided it was easier and more acceptable to practitioners to identify an *existing*, well-understood and well-accepted board that could be infused with statutory jurisdiction to hear and adjudicate tax foreclosure cases.

After much consideration, the board of revision was identified as best suited to hear foreclosure cases on vacant and abandoned properties. The board of revision in each county is recognized as a familiar, statutorily prescribed, functioning board that hears tax valuation cases, with guidelines concerning real estate valuation. The qualifications, the process, tenure, and duties of the board of revision members and their subordinate panels were all well-prescribed and established in law.

The next consideration, equally important, was whether this new expedited process should apply to all tax foreclosures or just vacant and abandoned properties. Since this entire effort was to allow communities to deal quickly with vacant and abandoned properties and repurpose them for productive reuse, it made sense for this new process to apply only to vacant and abandoned properties. Moreover, Treasurer Rokakis did not wish to apply expedited tax foreclosure to occupied properties because there could be many reasons why an occupied property has become tax delinquent. It could be the death of a property owner or spouse, the loss of employment, etc. In the case of a tax foreclosure of occupied properties, Jim felt it was best that these cases continue to be heard through the judicial foreclosure process, which retained all the pre-trial and mediation practices. In the case of vacant and abandoned properties, the reforms would be aimed at property owners who had left their property to deteriorate, negatively affecting surrounding properties in the community, and delaying tax-producing status. The next couple months were dedicated to drafting the new language into the real estate tax enforcement and collection chapters of the Ohio Revised Code.

After several drafting revisions, the concept of administrative tax foreclosure was now in the form of a bill which the Ohio Legislative Services Commission had approved, and we were ready to enlist our General Assembly sponsor in the Ohio House. State Representative Sally Conway Kilbane was the perfect house member to carry this bill.

She was a highly regarded member of the Republican delegation of the Ohio House of Representatives. The Ohio legislature has been largely dominated by the Republican Party for all but four of the last thirty years. In order to change laws in Ohio, you must be able to work with the party in the majority.

Passing complex legislation to change generations of property tax laws regarding tax foreclosure processes was going to be difficult. For starters, it had to gain the support of other county treasurers. Jim and I attended many legislative committees of the Ohio County Treasurers Association to garner their support. Treasurers' attitudes towards Jim ranged from supportive to bemused to annoyed. He was turning their notion of what county treasurers could and should do on its head. First he pushed for tax lien sales in 1999, then created a linked deposit program, and now this.

Eventually, the treasurers came around. But the tougher hurdle was with the powerful Ohio Prosecuting Attorneys Association. Their lobbyist was a man who had served in that position for over thirty years. John Murphy was the irascible septuagenarian who believed this bill was not needed and would not be supported by county prosecutors. He promised not to lend any support from the Ohio Prosecuting Attorneys Association, but fortunately, did not lead an all-out assault to kill the bill. Murphy held this opinion regardless of the Legislative Services Commission's position, which opined the bill was legal, or the examples of other states that conducted administrative foreclosures. In the House, our primary sponsor, Representative Kilbane, was indefatigable, and we passed the bill by a 90-9 vote on May 10, 2006. We then battled in the Senate, where we eventually prevailed by a 26-7 vote. Governor Taft signed the bill and H.B. 294 became effective on September 28, 2006.

I wrote H.B. 294 in a way that would allow a municipality or a municipal land bank to strategically target properties that it wanted to acquire in the event no bidders stepped forward to bid at a sheriff's sale. This tracked pre-existing land bank statutes, albeit much more quickly. The bill that I drafted and that ultimately passed the General Assembly also gave the board of revision the authority in select cases to directly transfer tax foreclosed abandoned properties to municipal land banks without exposure to sale. This feature could be invoked where the tax impositions exceeded the auditor's value of the property for tax purposes. For purposes of making this determination on whether to make a direct transfer, the auditor's value was rebuttably presumed to be the value of the property. The theory for this feature was based on the premise that there was no real need to conduct wasteful sheriff's sales when the taxes exceeded the value of the property. In such cases, there would rarely, if ever, be a bidder. And, if the rebuttable presumption of value was ever in question, the owner could simply come to the hearing and contest the valuation, enter into a payment plan, pay the taxes, ask for a continuance, or seek other relief. While the statute provided this feature to protect owners, owners rarely appeared to begin with, let alone invoked this feature. On the contrary, the theory proved true: owners of abandoned properties very rarely appeared at the hearings. The same held true for subordinate lien holders. Use of the rebuttable presumption as to value was more an evidentiary device rather than a statement of true fair market value. True fair market value aside from the tax valuation could only be discerned by an independent appraisal. The reason for the device was because in order to make a finding that the taxes exceeded the value of the property, a finding based on a hearing would normally have to occur, but since the abandoning owner never showed up for the hearing, there could be no hearing on this question. Therefore, the evidentiary finding of value would be made by the failure to rebut the presumption of the auditor's valuation. In other words, an owner who failed to appear at the hearing, *a priori*, failed to rebut the presumption, thereby eliminating the need for a further evidentiary hearing on that point.

In 2014 we made amendments to H.B. 294 to provide that a direct transfer of an abandoned tax foreclosed property could occur without reference to auditor's value. We had no idea in 2006 how helpful this board of revision (BOR) tax foreclosure process would turn out to be for land banks in the future. This new statute laid the groundwork for the 2014 amendments allowing for broader direct transfer authority to land banks.

What is it about a tax foreclosure that cleanses the title from old uncollectible taxes, liens and ultimately the interests of the former owner? Under the old foreclosure system, in order to eliminate all liens, extinguish all delinquent taxes, and remove the rights to the property from the delinquent owner, the property has to be foreclosed upon and a decree of foreclosure issued. The property then had exposed to sale, bid upon by a third party, and purchased at a sheriff's sale, with all the taxes paid by the new buyer as a precondition to getting a sheriff's deed. Unlike private mortgage foreclosures, the minimum bid in tax foreclosure cases is always the taxes, assessments, penalties, and interest. The value of the property is not relevant nor is the amount of the subordinate liens. There is no "marshalling of liens" as in a private foreclosure. On the contrary, this minimum bid is statutory and non-negotiable by either the county or the property owner. That sale then gets reported back to the court that issued the decree whereupon the court "confirms" the sale. Once confirmed, all rights of the taxpayer and subordinate lienholders are statutorily forever extinguished. To achieve "confirmation," those steps are inextricably tied together. Up to the point of the "confirmation," a taxpayer could step forward at the last minute and redeem the property by paying all taxes, assessments, penalties, and interest. This right of a property owner is called the "equity of redemption" or the owner's "redemption right." It is an inchoate right that gives the property owner the last chance to avoid losing title to the property. Redemption is a rarity with vacant and abandoned properties—especially those where the delinquent taxes exceed the auditor's fair market value for tax collection purposes. Under the old system, if no bidder appears to bid on the property, a municipal land bank could ask for the property and the statute would deem the municipality to be the purchaser of the property. This would result in a transfer to a municipal land bank at no cost, with all the taxes and encumbrances extinguished from the title. If a municipal land bank elected not to ask for unsold properties, those properties would "forfeit" to the state of Ohio and be included on the auditor's List of Forfeited Properties. More on forfeited properties in a moment.

The 2014 amendments to H.B. 294 revolutionized how the redemption right would be extinguished for vacant and abandoned properties. If the treasurer invoked these amendments, an "alternative right of redemption" ("ARR") was established. The right to redeem would no longer be based on exposure to sheriff's sale, purchase, and a court confirmation. The ARR extinguished the redemption right as a function of *time*, not exposure to sheriff's sale. In other words, after a decree of foreclosure, if a vacant and abandoned property was not redeemed by the owner within forty-five days (later reduced to twenty-eight days) or the taxes exceeded the presumed fair market value, the property could be conveyed directly by the sheriff to a municipality or county land bank without exposure to sheriff's sale. After the expiration of the twenty-eight-day redemption period, the termination of the right of redemption was self-executing, having the same legal effect of a "confirmation." Invoking the ARR was in the discretion of the treasurers throughout the state. In counties that elected not to invoke the available direct transfer provisions, the properties would be exposed to sale at a conventional sheriff's sale. Up to that point, the law required two exposures to sale, but it was changed in 2014 to require one sale if the property was vacant and abandoned.

The ARR turned tax foreclosure of abandoned properties into a highly strategic and more calculated way of moving properties back into tax productivity, explained more in Chapter Five. As of this writing, Ohio remains the only state in the country with this "redemption" feature.

So, what about those tax foreclosed properties that no one bids on and a land bank elects not to acquire? In such instances the property would "forfeit" to the State of Ohio. Under this process, called "state forfeiture," the property would escheat to the state, but only in the sense of a placeholder entity. The state is not required to take actual fee ownership of these properties, maintain them, or assume liability for any of the obligations or responsibilities of the forfeited property. The state is sovereign and not responsible to any local government for any aspect of the property, nor subject to municipal code violations. In my experience, except in rare circumstances, nothing is worse than this legal limbo title status because as a practical matter, no one is obligated to maintain or pay taxes on the property. The owner has abandoned the property. The only way these properties can be transacted is through periodic auditor's sales. Depending on the county, auditor's sales occur one or more times annually. Unlike at a sheriff's sale which is subject to the statutory minimum bid, at these auctions, the property typically sells for a fraction of the taxes. In many cases, they don't even sell at auditors' sales because of environmental or other property distress factors. In any case, these sales do nothing more than encourage speculation and predatory behavior that ultimately delays the long-term responsible repurposing of the property.

We knew H.B. 294 was no panacea, but it recognized the importance of expediting tax foreclosures, especially when properties posed a destabilizing influence in the community. They posed a "double whammy" to the public—crime and blight coupled with no tax collection. For the first time in Ohio, these properties could now be addressed expeditiously (in some cases four months from the date of filing the complaint with the BOR) and placed into traditional municipal land banks where they might remain sometimes for decades. That was 2006. By 2014 however, H.B.294 as amended would become a powerful tool in response to the new "land banks on steroids" which emerged in 2009.

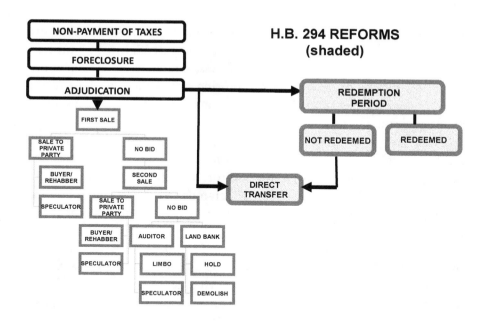

Getting H.B. 294 passed was only half of the battle. We now had a new law that had never been used. There was no context where we could do experimental dry runs to test all the administrative functions touching on tax foreclosure. We had no procedures in place other than the statute itself. The courts in Cuyahoga County were unfamiliar with the new law. New forms had to be created. Prosecutors had to be trained. At Jim's request I agreed to shift from a strict policy advisor role to the administrator of the H.B. 294 foreclosures. After developing adjudication and practice forms and case preparation rules, and establishing who would be the BOR members assigned to hear cases, the first foreclosures under the new law were filed in October 2006, and involved approximately thirty-four cases. Cases were filed with the clerk of courts by the foreclosure prosecutors. The clerk of court served all defendants consistent with Civil Rule 4 of the Rules of Civil Procedure along with a subsequent notice of final hearing. Notice of the final hearing dates in cases where defendants were served by publication was contained in the publication notice itself. This was later modified in 2014 to require defendants served by publication to file answers to the foreclosure filing within 28 days. As expected, not a single property owner and only a handful of subordinate lienholders showed up at the hearings, none of which stepped up to pay the delinquent taxes. A few bank mortgagees showed up to inquire about the new administrative procedure. In anticipation of a robust use of the new H.B. 294 process, I prepared a compendium of practice forms, sample adjudication forms, guidelines for the board of revision, hearing notice modifications of the clerk of court docket, and sheriff conveyance forms to be used by other counties electing to invoke BOR tax foreclosures.

The law was finally passed and working, but much of the implementation on a practical level within each county office required the buy-in and coordination of the auditor, treasurer, prosecutor, clerk of courts, and sheriff. There were dozens of granular modifications to internal practices in these offices. To the great credit of these administrators, they made H.B. 294 work.

Since that first hearing in 2006, over 17,000 cases have been heard through H.B. 294 proceedings in Cuyahoga County. An additional fifteen counties use H.B. 294 to foreclose on tax delinquent properties. We had no idea that the ability to foreclose quickly on abandoned and tax delinquent properties would be critical in the future, as funding for demolition would require quick turnaround on these foreclosures. H.B. 294 gave us an additional vehicle that one day could move properties into the yet-to-be formed county land banks.

Chapter Four:
"We're On Our Own"

> "We are at the mercy of international banks, national banks, an indifferent Congress, and a State Government that not only doesn't want to help us—but preempts us when we try to help ourselves."
> —*Cleveland Housing Court Judge Raymond Pianka, December 2008*

Jim Rokakis

We were thrilled to pass H.B. 294, which gave us a new and powerful tool to foreclose on tax delinquent, vacant, and abandoned properties, but 2006 and 2007 were especially difficult years in Cuyahoga County and Cleveland in particular. Mortgage foreclosures in those two years were the worst in the history of the county. Foreclosures reached 13,943 in 2006 and increased to 14,946 in 2007. As the heat maps below indicate, the foreclosure crisis had expanded from the city of Cleveland to the inner-ring suburbs—and beyond. Ultimately, only the most exclusive of Cleveland's suburbs— Hunting Valley and Gates Mills—escaped the foreclosure epidemic.

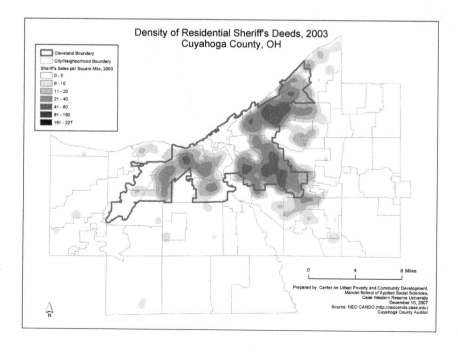

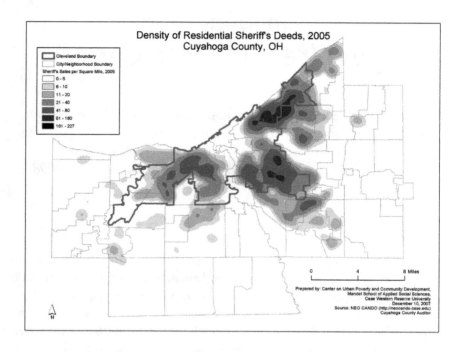

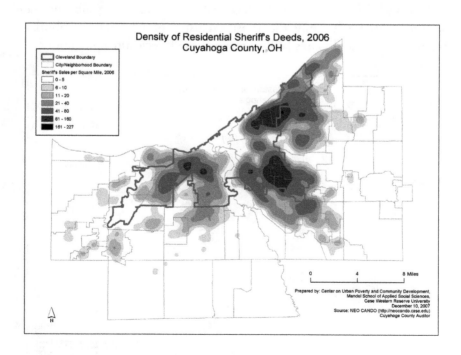

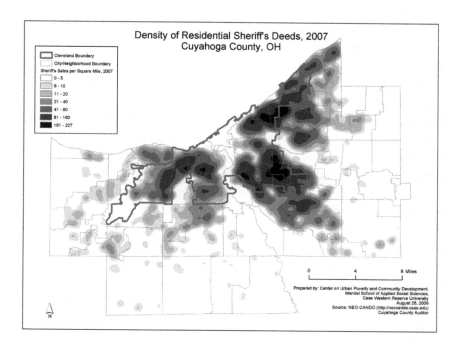

Density of Residential Sheriff's Deeds, 2007
Cuyahoga County, OH

Cleveland Boundary
City/Neighborhood Boundary
Sheriff's Sales per Square Mile, 2007
0 - 5
6 - 10
11 - 20
21 - 40
41 - 80
81 - 160
161 - 227

0   4   8 Miles

Prepared by: Center on Urban Poverty and Community Development,
Mandel School of Applied Social Sciences,
Case Western Reserve University
August 26, 2009
Source: NEO CANDO (http://neocando.case.edu)
Cuyahoga County Auditor

Tax collections were suffering at the county treasurer's office. In 2006, over $30 million had gone uncollected on vacant and abandoned structures and lots in Cleveland. It was extremely difficult to collect taxes on properties that were being foreclosed, but then being quickly transferred to new owners, often through quitclaim deeds. At the county treasury we did an informal study that showed that once a property was foreclosed on the east side of Cleveland during the period 2000–2010, the chance of that property ever paying property taxes again was only 5 percent! But that wasn't just in Cuyahoga County. Tax delinquencies were up in every county throughout the state. In Montgomery County, the City of Dayton lost over $8.7 million in uncollected property taxes in 2006. In Columbus, Franklin County, this figure was estimated to be approximately $7.5 million that same year—though limited data leads researchers to believe that this real value may be much higher. Many smaller cities felt this burden of lost property taxes as well, often disproportionately. Lima, a city of approximately 11,000 people in Allen County, lost approximately $1.4 million in property taxes in 2006—a per capita loss nearly thirteen times greater than that experienced in Columbus.

Additional and unexpected problems began to emerge. We were beginning to see the emergence of "zombie properties." This term referred to properties where a foreclosure was initiated by the financial institution and the legal owner of property abandoned it. But mortgage banks—the equitable owners upon an adjudication of foreclosure—were flooded with vacant and "underwater" properties that had mortgages that exceeded the actual value of the property. These banks were making decisions to either hold up acceptance of a sheriff's deed, or suspend the foreclosure action since they didn't want to take title to an abandoned, vandalized property. Or, once foreclosed judicially, they would not complete the "praecipe book" notifying the clerk and the sheriff to schedule the property for a sheriff's sale, which would leave the property in a kind of legal limbo. If the property had been exposed to sale, banks would not bid their own liens. They did this— and are still doing it—in order to avoid becoming stuck with a dilapidated property with no collateral value. This was not happening in stable or affluent neighborhoods, as banks knew that foreclosure and possession of that property could result in a quick resale and recovery of their initial investment. These "zombie properties" were commonplace throughout the county, and especially on Cleveland's east side, and were a real hindrance to recovery. And, in the early stages where banks had inadvertently bid their liens and acquired an abandoned property, they would quickly flip it to an unsophisticated or predatory speculator to avoid having to pay for the taxes, insurance and maintenance for what was to them a valueless property. They wanted to get it off their books and put the problem on the "books" of neighbors and taxpayers.

The federal government, through the Department of Housing and Urban Development (HUD), the Federal National Mortgage Association (FNMA), and the Federal Home Loan Mortgage Corporation (Freddie Mac), was adding to the problem by taking back tens of thousands of mortgages and selling—some would say flipping—them back to the market in bulk, often in groupings of thousands of mortgages at a time. In our experience, investors who purchased these were "cherry picking." They were keeping the best of these properties, or marketing them individually and reselling them on the market. They sold more troubled, low-value residences, often in Cleveland's distressed neighborhoods, for as little as $500 each. These distressed sales only added to the chaos as these bargain properties were rarely rehabilitated, thereby thoroughly corrupting the real value of properties for purposes of determining comparable values of surrounding properties. Cleveland City Councilman Jay Westbrook told the story of a man named Oswan Jackson, an unsophisticated buyer who purchased one of these homes in Cleveland's Stockyards neighborhood.

His wife was expecting, and he hoped to move his new family into the house. He paid $24,580 for a house through a land contract. The down payment was $500 and the payments were $290 per month. But after he purchased the home he learned that the city had already condemned it. As he began to rehabilitate the property he got another surprise—it carried $4,000 in unpaid property taxes. He walked away from the house.

In his article about Cleveland and the foreclosure crisis for *The New York Times Magazine*, Alex Kotlowitz told the story of Luis Jiminez, a train conductor from Long Beach, California, and the home he had purchased in Slavic Village—on eBay. He paid $4,000 for the house, but unbeknownst to him the house had been empty for two years, and had been completely stripped of its mechanicals, including the furnace and all the piping. The house was also condemned, and when Jiminez came to Cleveland to view his "investment" he decided to walk away.

I remember receiving an email in the treasurer's office from a physician who lived outside of London, England. He had purchased three homes on Cleveland's east side and expressed concern that one of the three properties was "missing." I spoke with him and learned he had purchased three vacant homes on eBay from a woman from South Carolina for more than $30,000. She picked them up in a HUD auction and immediately posted them on eBay. This poor man purchased them based on photos on the internet. The house that he said was missing had in fact been demolished by the city, as it had been condemned. Two weeks after we spoke, another one of those homes was demolished, as it too had been condemned. He had been duped, but I had little sympathy for somebody who bought property thousands of miles away, sight unseen, for what he described to me as one of his retirement strategies.

The collapse of the real estate market on the east side of Cleveland was manifesting itself in another shocking and quantifiable statistic: population loss in the city. Census figures put Cleveland's population in 2000 at approximately 480,000 people. As houses became vacant, the population in the city took a nosedive. Houses coming off-line were not being rehabilitated. They were dead—permanently vacant. By 2005 the population was less than 415,000. The number dropped to 406,000 by 2006. Much of the city was emptying out.

Five years had passed since I approached the Federal Reserve Bank of Cleveland. Tens of thousands of properties had been foreclosed. By this point I was convinced that the evidence of wide-scale fraud was sufficient enough for us to convene a group of state and federal agencies and begin an investigation, with accompanying prosecutions that would, once and for all, slow down the runaway train of reckless lending and speculation. Highly publicized prosecutions and jail terms for corrupt players in the mortgage industry would have a chilling effect on their behavior. I contacted the U.S. Attorney for the Northern District of Ohio, Greg White, and requested a meeting. I requested that attendees include postal inspectors, FBI agents, U.S. attorneys from his office, and a representative of the local county prosecutor, Bob Coury. At this meeting, we brought a convincing case against real estate fraud involving Argent Mortgage. Its destructive behavior was taking a toll on Cleveland and Cuyahoga County every day. Argent Mortgage would be an easy target, we thought, for prosecutors.

At that meeting we showed the prosecutor and others that Argent was issuing mortgages for at least 200 percent of county auditor's value and demonstrated that many of those mortgages were being foreclosed upon within ninety days. Fraud was rampant. We asked the U.S. Attorney's office to lead the charge and prosecute Arnall and his minions in what we believed was an organized criminal conspiracy. We asked U.S. Attorney White to look at the behavior of Arnall and his organization under the Racketeer Influenced and Corrupt Organizations Act (RICO), a federal statute that allows federal prosecutors to bring civil and criminal charges against leaders of an organization for ordering others to commit criminal acts. We argued that the wide scale fraud by low level mortgage brokers at Argent did not happen without the direction of higher-ups at Argent—including Arnall himself.

I struck out at that meeting, just as I had with the Federal Reserve Bank several years earlier. U.S. Attorney White explained to me that because of the attacks on 9/11, he and many federal investigators were tied up in seeking out terrorist threats and ensuring there would not be any repeat tragedies. I understood why U.S. Attorney White said he could not commit resources, but what I could not understand was the comment of one U.S. attorney who asked me why Argent Mortgage wasn't in the room, since they appeared to be the victim of fraudulent mortgages. He didn't get it. I had just spent the better part of an hour explaining to him that Argent—and its army of mortgage brokers—was the perpetrator of the crime and not the victim. But my answer left him cold. I left this meeting like so many others—discouraged, and with the realization that no one was going to step up to assist us in our efforts.

Ironically, the failure of the federal government to step up and deal with this problem opened other doors. The Cuyahoga County Prosecutor's office, led by then-prosecutor Bill Mason, began to take a more active role in the prosecution of mortgage fraud—and began to receive a steady stream of referrals from frustrated FBI agents, because the U.S. Attorney's office was expressing reluctance to commit resources and pursue mortgage foreclosure fraud. Former Cuyahoga County Common Pleas Court Judge Michael Jackson started at the prosecutor's office in late 2006 as a special prosecutor investigating mortgage fraud. Jackson was an attorney in private practice who had done a number of pro bono bankruptcies for people who were caught in mortgage foreclosures. Many of his clients were people who were financially unsophisticated, and got trapped in mortgages that they could not pay. He responded to a request at a continuing legal education conference made by the prosecutor's office to go after mortgage fraud. Within six months of being hired, with the assistance of the of the Cuyahoga County Sheriff's Department, Jackson had assembled thousands of documents and moved forward on over fifty indictments, indicting seventy-five defendants in mortgage fraud. Before he left that office in 2012 after being elected judge, over 250 individuals had been indicted by the county prosecutor's office. Unfortunately, much of the damage in mortgage foreclosure fraud was done several years before the mortgage foreclosure fraud unit was even established, but the prosecutor's office did make an effort to shut these corrupt practices down.

We were making progress with H.B. 294 moving more quickly on foreclosures of vacant and abandoned property, and with foreclosure prevention efforts assisting hundreds of homeowners. Prosecutors were finally starting to take notice of criminal activity and prosecuting the worst of the offenders locally. But the overall real estate picture was still one of chaos—and to make matters worse we were in the beginning stages of a financial crisis caused by the collapse of the mortgage market. The Great Recession was upon us.

We needed to do more.

VAPAC and Housing Court Judge Ray Pianka continued to talk about the need for additional tools—like the powerful county land bank pioneered by County Treasurer Dan Kildee in Genesee County, Michigan— in Cuyahoga County. The judge felt the trauma of the foreclosure crisis more acutely than anyone. Each day his courtroom was flooded by a cast of characters, property owners and speculators from all over the country. He was taking a hard line position against many of these bad actors. In fact, the term "Pianka'd" became popular, as speculators and bad landlords and banks that went before Judge Pianka smarted from the stern lecture and steep fine they invariably received.

But the judge recognized the futility of his efforts. This was an international financial meltdown, and we were trying to beat it alone. We were losing that fight. I remember hearing Ray say to a group of us at a meeting in his office: "We are at the mercy of international banks, national banks, an indifferent congress and a state government that not only doesn't want to help us—but preempts us when we try to help ourselves."

He had been paying close attention to the Genesee County Land Bank. We all knew about municipal land banks, which had been around since the early 1980s. These municipal land banks were nothing more than a "holding tank"—a repository for vacant lands—for municipal governments. While held in these land banks they were exempt from property taxes. But there was no special funding mechanism for these municipal land banks, and the thousands of properties being held by the City of Cleveland were costing the city millions annually in maintenance costs. The county land bank in Genesee, however, was different. For starters it had a funding mechanism—a dedicated stream of revenue to help alleviate the costs of maintaining the many properties it owned. And, although only several years old, it was taking control of thousands of properties in and around Flint, Michigan, the distressed city that made up the core of that county. We had to see it ourselves.

A group of us ventured up to Flint to visit Kildee and see his operation first hand. We invited him to Cleveland as well, and we exchanged notes about what he had done and what we needed to do here in Cuyahoga County and in the State of Ohio to deal with the scourge of vacant and abandoned properties. A number of attorneys looked at the Michigan law and opined on what would be required to create a strong Ohio law, including Kermit Lind—then a law professor at Cleveland-Marshall College of Law—and Frank Ford. But ultimately the responsibility for writing the Ohio land bank law would fall on Gus Frangos. Once again, we called on him to use the Michigan law as a model in drafting a bill in Ohio that would give us the kind of authority that the Genesee County Land Bank had—and perhaps more. He wrote a bill that the Dean of Emory Law School and an expert of the land bank movement, Frank Alexander, called "an incredibly complex and sophisticated masterpiece that wove intricate connections among tax foreclosure, tax penalties and revenues, municipal powers, not-for-profit corporation powers, property acquisition, management, and disposition authority, and intergovernmental collaboration." This bill was even more complicated than H.B. 294. Again, the drafter of the bill explains it best.

Chapter Five:
Senate Bill 353

"Senate Bill 353 . . . an incredibly complex and
sophisticated masterpiece."
—Frank Alexander, Sam Nunn Professor of Law, Emory University
School of Law, 2015

Gus Frangos

The successful implementation of H.B. 294 expedited tax foreclosures in Cuyahoga County, resulting in more and more cases being filed in the board of revision as tax foreclosure dockets steadily increased. By 2008 and 2009, tax foreclosures of vacant and abandoned properties had skyrocketed. With the massive increase in board of revision tax foreclosure cases being filed, and prospects of thousands more to follow, the county needed a responsible repository to acquire and manage these properties and the resulting chaos. Up to that point, these tax-foreclosed properties were exposed to sheriff's sale and typically sold to speculators or, if the property was without a bidder after exposure to sale, ultimately forfeited to the state. In some cases, a property would directly transfer to a municipality without exposure to a sheriff's sale where the tax impositions exceeded the auditor's tax assessed value. Typically, this happened with vacant lots as opposed to structures. As these properties remained vacant and abandoned, they burdened municipalities and had detrimental effects on neighboring properties. Jim Rokakis wanted to address this problem.

Jim was aware of the work pioneered by Genesee County Treasurer Dan Kildee (now Congressman Dan Kildee from Michigan's Fifth District), who had conceptualized the first county land banks. These Michigan land banks were far more transactional and effective than the traditional passive land banks of municipalities in Ohio. Jim asked me to consult with Dan on the structure of the Genesee County Land Bank model. Dan's input and experience guided our planning immensely—county land banks were no longer an abstract concept, but a tangible goal.

For this process to be successful, the new practice of land banking needed to be, as much as possible, a seamless overlay on existing land banking and county practices, while containing much needed transactional reforms. Once again, this overlay needed to incorporate the six county agencies involved in tax foreclosure and land use. These agencies would again need to buy in to all the changes in order to implement the new reforms we were about to propose. To start with, H.B. 294 (tax foreclosure practice) would need to be woven into any land bank legislation. Not only would the county land banks serve as a responsible repository for foreclosed, abandoned properties, but they also needed the acquisition pipeline to vacant and abandoned properties that H.B. 294 afforded. In other words, tax foreclosure needed to have a dual function—tax collection and more broadly, community development.

We established a small working group to draft the legislation that would make this possible. I persuaded Jim to have the group focus primarily on creating the "legal schematics" while deferring consideration of "operational schematics." Operational schematics would become more relevant once the land bank legislation drafting was well under way. This small working group swelled, at one point, to several dozen people.

Several community meetings followed, and there came a point when I felt these meetings were becoming counterproductive. While attendees provided plenty of valuable input, one particular meeting devolved into complaints about entirely unrelated issues. As the meeting concluded, I suggested to everyone that they allow me to prepare a focused, legislative synopsis that could serve as a broad, aspirational working document. I asked, "If Dorothy could click her heels and wish for a land bank, what would that land bank look like and what issues would it address?" Everyone agreed. I prepared what is now known as the "Dorothy Memo," which summarized the input of the working group. In truth, there was nothing new in the memo. Rather, it captured what community development advocates, councilpersons, and code enforcers had been advocating and working on for years--things that I had also learned serving as a Cleveland city councilman. It nevertheless asserted the group consensus and allowed us to move on to drafting what would soon become S.B. 353.

Jim retained municipal finance attorney Robert (Bob) Rink to work with me in researching and crafting legislation that would design these new entities. Kermit Lind, a clinical professor of law emeritus at Cleveland-Marshall College of Law, also brainstormed with us early on. Kermit was an advocate for predatory lending reforms and accountability, and taught code enforcement practice and public interest law at the law clinic he supervised. We affirmed three necessary components for successful land bank legislation. The first was identifying consistent and sufficient funding sources. Without reliable funding, the effort was futile. The second was identifying the appropriate type of entity and the breadth of its powers. This entity needed to be a public purposed entity residing outside of government in order to allow for flexible and entrepreneurial transactional capabilities. The third was the extraordinary task of weaving in H.B. 294 tax foreclosure reform. Without a direct and meaningful pipeline to the vacant and abandoned properties through tax foreclosure, any attempt at removing blight and repurposing properties would, at best, be tepid.

In those early days, Jim and I attended Cuyahoga County Mayors and City Managers Association meetings to explain our approach and gain acceptance particularly regarding the funding method. As the foreclosure crisis began to encroach into the outer-ring suburbs (and was no longer just an urban issue), most mayors and managers embraced the concept. While some remained reticent, and at least one outright opposed it, the group substantially viewed county land banks as a reasonable way to address the foreclosure crisis.

In order to identify funding sources, Jim and I had numerous conversations with then-Genesee County Treasurer Dan Kildee about how that county funded its land bank under Michigan law. We discovered that Michigan land bank law provided a funding mechanism for its land banks but not in sufficient amount to meet the daunting task they had to deal with. Genesee's land bank acquired thousands of properties without the ability to effectively triage, maintain, and quickly but responsibly dispose of properties. At one point, this led Flint Mayor Dayne Walling in 2011 to unfairly criticize the land bank's maintenance practices. "It is not acceptable for the foreclosed properties to go without basic upkeep and maintenance," he said. "The purpose of the Land Bank is to keep the properties in better condition than if they were owned by out-of-town landlords." This was unfair in that the Genesee County Land Bank was a public repository of last resort that provided a modicum of maintenance, helped dispose of properties responsibly and generally kept these properties out of the hands of speculators and unwholesome flippers.

What ultimately emerged from these discussions with Dan included a little bit of "what to do, and what not to do." Our concept for funding and property acquisition was twofold: (1) we would explore recapture of penalty and interest on delinquent tax collections, and redirect that revenue to county land banks as a source of reliable funding; and (2) we would devise a system which allowed county land banks to choose strategically which tax foreclosed properties to acquire based on funding, capacity, and community priorities. This kind of calibrated acquisition strategy would not only promote catalytic dispositions but also avoid the kind of criticism of Flint's Mayor Walling. It should be pointed out that in the aftermath of the foreclosure crisis, cities across the nation were struggling with this problem. This is why it was unfortunate for Mayor Walling to criticize the Genesee County Land Bank.

Our first task was to determine a method of diverting penalties and interest to the land bank in a way that would make sense to the taxing districts. Rink and I spoke with Chief Deputy Treasurer Robin Darden Thomas about making bookkeeping advances of anticipated delinquent tax collections so that the taxing districts would receive funds earlier in the tax cycle. If the treasurer's office could forecast the rate of collection of the overall delinquency in its taxing districts, the treasurer could use its active funds on deposit to advance a portion of the anticipated delinquent collections. In this way, the advance payment would be deemed as paid on-time as far as the taxing districts were concerned. In effect, this had the effect of paying the taxing district within the normal settlement period, but redirecting penalties and interest, which would be set aside for county land bank use.

Bob Rink was the former finance director for the City of Cleveland Heights, and was very adept at public finance, particularly county and municipal financing. Bob was also the author of the Ohio tax lien certificate law adopted by the Ohio General Assembly in the 1990s, codified as R.C. 5721.30 to R.C. 5721.40. With this background, Bob crafted R.C. 133.082, calling for the sale of tax anticipation securities; and RC. 133.341, calling for tax anticipation lines of credit and tax-forecasted advances of anticipated tax delinquent collections to taxing districts which would result in the capture and setting apart of the tax penalty and interest. The amendments as written did not actually mandate the advance payment to the taxing districts, but the concept gave county treasurers the discretion to make the earlier distribution and retain the penalties and interest for county land bank use. This process was simpler and less costly than issuing tax anticipation securities, which required the full faith and credit of the county to guarantee such an issuance. Though unknown at the time, these methods would not turn out to be the easiest ways of funding county land banks.

These sections did essentially three things: (1) authorized the issuing of tax anticipation notes as securities; (2) allowed for the simple forecasting and advancing of unpaid and delinquent taxes to taxing districts from active funds on deposit with the treasurer; and (3) made these advances available to the taxing districts within a few weeks following the biannual collection, while retaining the penalty and interest for county land banks. These procedures required a good amount of analysis to make sure the advances were not too inflated which would make it harder to recover the advances or paying off any debt instruments used to make the advances.

While I was assigned to craft the legislation, I was not a finance expert. I was a transactional attorney, and my experience was in real estate and business transactions. My role was to add the necessary enhancements and features to the tax foreclosure process, define our unique governance, and enable the transactional elements of the legislation that *transactionally* addressed the problem we were trying to solve. I felt the "tax advance" system could produce disparate methodology in tax collection throughout the counties of the state and had inherent uncertainties associated with forecasting future delinquent tax collections. I was concerned with the entire concept of tax anticipation advances and having to interact with the numerous taxing districts to manage these advances. This process might prove too unwieldy and risk the loss of buy-in from the taxing districts. Nevertheless, because Ohio counties don't officially budget for penalty and interest collections, this was an opportunity to make sure these funds were isolated for land bank use. Indeed, in many other states, penalty and interest, once collected, is in fact budgeted as a form of "miscellaneous" income which taxing districts anticipate in future budget cycles. In those states, any attempt to isolate "penalty and interest" would be viewed as encroaching on taxing district budgets.

Because penalty and interest is not budgeted in Ohio, I advocated for an alternative to the advance payment concept. This would be a simplified and uniform method embedded into the tax collection statutes for those counties choosing to establish county land banks. There was a county fund called the Delinquent Tax and Assessment Collection (DTAC) fund. When any delinquent taxes were collected by the treasurer, 5 percent of that overall collection (including a portion of the 10 percent penalty on that delinquent collection) would be set aside for prosecutor's and treasurer's offices to fund the continued tax collection and enforcement efforts of their respective offices. One half of that amount (2.5 percent) is directed to the county prosecutor to help pay for tax foreclosure prosecution and related costs. It covers everything from the prosecutor's staff, preliminary judicial reports, filing fees, publication notices, etc. The other 2.5 percent is dedicated to the county treasurer for public collection notices, legally required advertising of delinquencies, postage, maintaining a collection staff, and generally managing the collection of delinquent taxes. I proposed that the new land bank legislation include an additional 5 percent fee increase on the DTAC to be set aside and allocated specifically for county land bank operations. Since all collected delinquent taxes included a 10 percent penalty added to the actual tax corpus, the penalty on delinquencies would be sufficient to cover the additional 5 percent to be added to the existing 5 percent DTAC fee. The 10 percent penalty applied to the actual tax corpus would substantially preserve the budgeted, levied, or voted taxes of the taxing districts and not result in an encroachment on the actual corpus thereof. In other words, the taxing districts would receive *all* of their budgeted tax corpus. They just would not receive all of the penalty and interest derived from the overall delinquent payment.

In Cuyahoga County, this method produces between $7 million to $9 million annually. The Cuyahoga County Council capped our revenue at $7 million. The ability to have an identifiable and reliable source of funding, regardless of the amount, allows land banks to fully pursue all the enablements provided in the land bank statute. It allows them to create budgets, set priorities, and hire professional staff consistent with their DTAC allocation in their respective counties. This then allows land banks to establish longstanding programs and promotes quality hiring. Bob Rink incorporated the 5 percent DTAC increase into the DTAC statute, and this is the source of revenue for all county land banks in Ohio.

As to choice of entity, Kermit, Bob, and I initially contemplated creating a public authority that could levy and receive taxes, float bonds, and otherwise serve as a taxing district to which taxes could be directed. The entity could hold property exempt from real estate taxes. As quickly as we suggested creating a public authority, it was dismissed for several reasons. Creating a public authority would essentially create another layer of government. The demands of the situation required transactions to be quick, aggressive, and flexible, much like in private enterprise. Governments are often not able to transact in that manner. Moreover, creating such an entity would be a lengthy process, and would require more regulated expenditure authority and governance complexities, and invoke the very systems and impediments in government that we were trying to streamline.

We decided that the appropriate entity would be a community improvement corporation (CIC). Title 17 of the Ohio Revised Code is the corporate "entity" chapter within the Ohio Revised Code. It provides for every variety of entity, from non-profit corporations to partnerships to LLCs, medical corporations, associations and the traditional for-profit corporations. The CIC is a unique blend of a public purposed entity without being a governmental unit. Many counties and cities in Ohio have established CIC's for the various purposes deemed necessary by the political subdivision creating it. It is, in every respect, a non-profit corporation but with public features. The statute envisions these public purpose corporations to focus traditionally on one or more *economic development or industrial development* activities. As long as the CIC is operating within its county-prescribed purpose, the statute allows these corporations to do virtually everything that a for-profit corporation can. We added a third wholly new category of CIC called county land reutilization corporations, or county land banks for short. These entities would have the same nature and the transactional capabilities of a conventional CIC, but these corporations would also be endowed with the powers of traditional land banks under R.C. 5722. We implanted R.C. 5722 land banks onto these new R.C. 1724 CICs. In other words, the county would create a land bank for itself, but through the agency and instrumentality of a modified community improvement corporation.

It should be noted that a CIC is sometimes difficult to define depending on the context. Several Ohio Attorney General opinions have attempted to characterize a CIC. A smattering of Courts and Ohio Attorney General opinions define the CIC as a non-profit entity distinct from government but tied to the government creating it. Its contracts and liabilities are independent of the county and may not be visited upon the county that created it unless the county chooses to accept that responsibility. There is no *respondeat superior* liability between a government creating a CIC and the CIC itself. In this respect, a CIC is considered an "agent" of a county, but more like an independent contractor without creating vicarious liabilities upon the county. CICs are private non-profit corporations with public attributes. The public attributes of CIC's are that they are created by a political subdivision, and that they are subject to open records laws, open meeting laws, and audit by the state. At least one Ohio Attorney General opinion relentingly characterizes CICs as private entities but concludes that they are a "hybrid." Recently, the bidding practices of the Trumbull County Land Bank were challenged. The challenge asserted that any bidding practices needed to be performed in accordance with Sections 307.86 and 307.92 of the Ohio Revised Code since county land banks were alleged to be "political subdivisions." The Eleventh District Court of Appeals disagreed and affirmed that county land banks are independent, private CICs and not subject to these procurement standards. This case was then further appealed to the Ohio Supreme Court, which denied a writ of certiorari.

Bob and I amended Chapter 1724 of the Ohio Revised Code so that county land banks can also serve as "electing subdivisions" as defined in the traditional land bank statute. "Electing subdivisions" are traditional "land banks" under the Chapter 5722 of the Revised Code, which was enacted in the 1970s to allow municipalities and select political subdivisions to "elect" to have a land bank. Up to this point, electing subdivisions were exclusively governmental bureaus or departments within a political subdivision. We changed that by extending these governmental powers to this new category of CICs while leaving behind most of the bureaucratic restrictions on expedient property and business transactions This new type of CIC which I will refer to as a county land bank would be able to hold property tax exempt like a traditional land bank, be governed by an independent board, receive properties from tax foreclosure, buy and sell properties, and invest and collaborate with other non-profits and private enterprises to repurpose distressed property and promote the tax base in a highly nimble and transactional manner.

Property under government control might require ordinance authority, multiple planning reviews, board of control scheduling, council approvals, etc. in order to transact. With county land banks, the corporation's board would create and define its own broad guidelines within which staff could transact so that board action would not be required for every transaction, conveyance, acquisition, sale, disposition, and vendor relationship.

Incorporating H.B. 294 and Other Modifications

At this point, two of the three necessary broad legislative components had been conceptually identified and agreed to. We had identified funding options and a flexible, transactional non-profit entity to serve as the operating vehicle. These R.C. 1724 corporations would serve as "land banks on steroids," as stated by then-Genesee County Treasurer Dan Kildee.

The third component involved the intricate task of weaving H.B. 294 tax foreclosures into the county land bank legislation. Virtually every tax chapter in the Ohio Revised Code relating to real estate, tax exemption, and land banking had to be modified to do this. This was critical, as tax foreclosure would become the major pipeline to acquiring title-cleared vacant and abandoned land. Creating a system of marketable title through tax foreclosure was critical. No matter how many properties could be acquired by a county land bank, if it could not transact to third parties with marketable and insurable titles, land banks would sputter just to transact a few properties at a time. An efficient land bank, however, would need to transact hundreds and thousands of properties over time.

Accordingly, as we drafted the legislation, the conventional tax foreclosure statutes were all modified to allow for transfers to county land banks in an expedient manner. For example, rather than two sheriff's sales, a vacant and abandoned property need only be exposed to one sale. When the tax impositions exceeded the auditor's presumed fair market value of the property, such properties, at the request of a county land bank, could be transferred directly to a county or municipal land bank without exposure to sale. This drastically shortened the time frames for tax foreclosure dispositions.

Another significant enablement came in the tax forfeiture statute. Once a property was exposed to sale without a bidder, the property would be forfeited to the state as described in Chapter Three. The property would stay in this limbo status while the title remained clouded, simply because the original owner still retained the so-called "right of redemption." Only when the auditor auctioned these state-forfeited properties would this right of redemption terminate as a matter of law. The land bank bill provided a means by which county land banks could obtain properties that were on the tax forfeiture list by simply making a written request. Additionally, because the quality of a property was always unknown and therefore a risky acquisition, the law was changed to provide that any property on the state forfeiture list could be legally inspected for environmental, code, and safety issues by a municipality and a county land bank. County land banks were immunized from liability for trespass or damage claims for this purpose. Once a property was thus claimed, title to the property would be conveyed to a county land bank (and any of its transferees), free and clear of all taxes, assessments, liens, and encumbrances.

Another important tool that we included in the land bank bill was the enhancement of the municipal nuisance abatement sections of the Revised Code (mainly R.C 715.26 and 715.261). These code sections allow municipalities to declare a nuisance on a dangerous property, and to either demolish it after a lengthy legal certification process, or cut the grass, remove debris, board it up and condemn such properties. The municipality could only enforce collection on these charges against the property owner by referring the charges to the county auditor as assessments onto the tax duplicate. However, municipalities did not have the ability to foreclose on their nuisance liens, and were instead dependent on county prosecutors to file tax foreclosure actions. The enhancement to these sections gave municipalities and county land banks the ability to assert liens not only onto the tax duplicate, but gave them new authority to file separate liens that could be foreclosed upon independently by the municipalities and county land banks. By doing this, municipal land banks could more efficiently acquire vacant and abandoned properties, find responsible owners, and place the property back onto productive status if they would so choose. If the municipality or county land bank did not want to acquire the property through foreclosure but still wanted to pursue collection for the nuisance abatement charges, the new amendments allowed them to pursue independent money damage lawsuits against the property owner. And if a property was uncollectible, these lawsuits could result in judgment liens against the property and the titled owner as in any other civil judgments.

A unique and important feature of the nuisance abatement sections authorized county land banks to step into the shoes of municipalities, by way of an "agency" agreement. Many municipalities throughout the state have the capacity to follow all of the statutory sequences of placing nuisance liens on a property, providing notice and then conducting nuisance abatement activity. However, in the wake of the foreclosure crisis, many smaller and rural communities around Cuyahoga County found this process new and cumbersome. They did not always have the expertise or the resources to conduct demolition and nuisance abatement activities with the attendant requirements of environmental surveys, asbestos abatement, transfer to regulated dump sites, etc.

In those instances, where county land banks would fund or receive funding from the municipality or an outside source, the municipality and county land banks could now execute an agency agreement to allow county land banks to conduct the nuisance abatement activities on behalf of municipalities. This differs from simply having a municipality sign a contract for demolition services. In nuisance abatement cases, the original owner who abandoned the property continues to be in title. As such, a county land bank as a separate entity is not automatically entitled to abate a nuisance on private property. Only cities with the police power of enforcement over nuisances can declare a property a nuisance and enter onto the property. By modifying Section 715.261, the "agency" relationship was not one of contract, but one of limited municipal authority being conferred upon land banks by virtue of statutory edict. This would allow for quick engagement, avoidance of lengthy procurement rules in cases of emergency, and arguably confer the municipality's sovereign immunity upon the county land bank in the individual case.

The original S.B. 353 also immunized county land banks from environmental liability so long as the county land bank did not commence development or disturb existing environmental conditions. This is an important environmental "safe harbor" applicable to Ohio EPA regulations. And, finally the 2014 amendments officially conferred sovereign immunity upon county land banks pursuant to Chapter 2744.01 et seq.

2014 Amendments

In 2014, many amendments were made to S.B. 353 and H.B. 294 that involved tweaks and enhancements born out of the benefit of experience after the bill's original passage in 2009. These amendments were embodied in S.B. 172. An example of such operations-based modifications to the bill included clarifying the status of municipal liens for nuisance abatement costs and how to treat these, and pre-existing water and sewer liens. For example, when a tax foreclosure occurs, are municipal nuisance abatement liens that were placed on the tax duplicate extinguished in the same way as private liens and encumbrances? And, importantly, what would happen after a tax foreclosure was completed and the property was transferred to a land bank, and later to a third party? If this responsible third party fully rehabilitated the property and was living in it, and then one year later a municipality placed an older water and sewer lien on the property for charges that predated the land bank's acquisition, how would this title issue be disentangled?

This problem beguiled every county land bank and created enormous issues for innocent renovators trying to disentangle the lien that would appear on a property seemingly out of nowhere. In the world of land banking and real estate, clear title is king. Happily, the statutes were changed to declare these municipal liens invalid to an acquiring county land bank and its transferees, provided that the nuisance or utility charges did not originate during the land bank's ownership. Such liens were eliminated, effective on the date of a recorded deed transfer to a county land bank whether they appeared of record prior to the transfer or were placed of record thereafter. The amendments also gave citizens the right to contact their county auditor and present a deed showing the date of transfer, which would give citizens a self-enforceable means of having these liens extinguished as a matter of law. I cannot emphasize enough the importance of addressing issues like this regarding the marketability and alienation of properties. Title marketability is at the core of repurposing properties and placing them back into productive use.

Other enhancements, while seemingly insignificant, were crucial to the volume of properties being tax foreclosed, transferred to land banks, and repurposed. Some of the enhancements simply dealt with ease of administration. One such example involved modifying the law to allow intergovernmental transfers between municipal and county land banks. Revised Code Chapter 5722, the original land banking statute, authorized the clearance of all taxes and the ability to hold properties tax exempt if acquired through tax foreclosure only. When a county land bank received a property through tax foreclosure, that would present no problem—the property could be held exempt from real estate taxes pending future productive disposition. However, if the county land bank demolished a blighted property and transferred the resulting vacant lot to a municipality which had its own land bank, such transfer to the municipal land bank from the county land bank was technically *not* the result of a tax foreclosure transfer and thereby required municipalities to file tax exemption applications for thousands of properties conveyed to them. This became an administrative problem fraught with the potential for error: forgetting to file the form on time, making mistakes on the form, etc. The laws were changed to allow transfers between county and municipal land banks and transfers to land banks from other sources to be treated as if they were acquired by tax foreclosure, and automatically exempted retroactive to the passage date of S.B. 353 in 2009. This negated the need for municipalities to file these cumbersome exemption forms (see R.C. 5709.12). Ultimately, the land bank bill contained numerous "bells and whistles" that would allow counties to interact, share services, and support county land banks in ways that would normally require some separate legislative authorization or contract.

The application of other bureaucratic features of the original 1970s municipal land bank legislation was made not applicable to the new county land banks. For example, a system of "consent" from taxing districts overlaying a particular land bank-acquired property was required. Technically, an overlaying taxing district would have to give its consent to allowing the municipality to take a property into its land bank inventory. Such an overlaying taxing district might include a library, RTA, Port Authority, schools, and the county itself. As a practical matter this is not done, or if done, is on an omnibus basis. The municipality technically has to maintain an accounting such that once a municipality sells a land bank property—in many cases years later--any net proceeds of the sale would have to be credited to the various other taxing districts overlaying the property that had been land banked. There would rarely ever be "net" proceeds after accounting for the municipality's maintenance and holding costs. In extremely rare instances in which a municipality or county land bank might recover more proceeds from the sale above the amount of taxes extinguished and holding costs over the years, the new amendments recognized that this recovery was inconsequential compared to the amount of sunken loss from holding and often demolishing thousands of other properties. The amendments eliminated this application for county land banks. As of this writing, a bill is in the works that will remove these bureaucratic "consents" for municipal land banks as well.

Another change had to do with advisory boards, which were intended to foster neighborhood input into land bank disposition decisions. This input was never defined in the 1970s statutes. We found this 1970s requirement unnecessary for county land banks because county land banks operate on a county level, and local community development and planning departments perform this function. This does not apply to county land banks and a bill is being developed to eliminate this requirement for municipalities.

After the first few years of operation, the Cuyahoga Land Bank presented the Cuyahoga County Council a report on the use of the additional 5 percent DTAC allotted to the Cuyahoga Land Bank to determine how much, if any, of this set-aside encroached on the budgeted tax revenues of any of the county's taxing districts. To this date with one or two minor exceptions (resulting from large institutional valuation disputes), the formula has held firm. The DTAC funding of land banks has not encroached upon direct tax corpus payable to the taxing districts. Because this 5 percent DTAC alternative was far easier to manage than tax advances and tax anticipation notes, this has become the standard throughout virtually all land banks in Ohio. Other states are trying to emulate this same funding mechanism for their land banks. To date Ohio is the only state in the country that employs this device.

Writing S.B. 353 and its subsequent amendments required a lot of research and harmonization of numerous sections and chapters of the Ohio Revised Code. Then-Senator Tom Patton was our sponsoring champion of both S.B. 353 and later S.B 172. When the Legislative Services Commission (LSC) was presented with our early drafts, we were allowed to interact directly with LSC attorneys with whom we maintained a good and professional working relationship. Tom Patton deserves many accolades for his contribution to the state's land banking system.

Once introduced as a bill, we had assembled support from many sectors—banking lobbyists, community development advocates, the media, and several statewide associations such as the County Auditors Association and County Treasurers Association. One group that opposed S.B. 353 was a group called OREIA (Ohio Real Estate Investors Association). OREIA was a private association of rehabbers and investors that either resold or rented properties. OREIA thought we were trying to become competitors with their membership in the rental business. Nothing could be further from the truth. After numerous meetings and "sidebars" at the statehouse with this group, we finally garnered their reluctant support.

Our bill started in the Ohio Senate. We assembled letters of support from community development practitioners and government officials throughout the state. We came to the State and Local Government Committee of the Senate chaired by then-Senator Gary Cates. We came prepared with graphs, tax collection timelines, diagrams of the foreclosure and tax collection process, and historical data regarding the effects of the financial crisis to stress the need for this legislation. We also recruited the pre-eminent land banking expert Frank Alexander, Dean of Emory University's law school in Atlanta, Georgia, to testify on behalf of the bill. Frank has written more than anyone in the nation on the subject of land banks, tax foreclosure, and land use. He has drafted land bank legislation himself for several states through his association with the Center for Community Progress. During his testimony, Frank described the bill as a masterpiece and a "national model." We could not have received a better endorsement. Committee Chairman Senator Gary Cates told us that ours was the most complete and professional presentation he had presided over during his Senate tenure. Having the committee chairman on your side was a good sign!

What made Senate Bill 353 unique is that this was not a singular bill parked in a new section or chapter of the Ohio Revised Code creating land banks on paper alone; on the contrary, it involved the highly surgical amending and harmonizing of hundreds of sections of the Revised Code so that all of the aforesaid six county agencies, along with budget commissions, cities, and the county itself were aligned for tax foreclosure purposes and actual land banking practice.

Our bill passed the Senate committee with flying colors and we thought we were on our way. At the last minute, one senator was apprehensive about infusing so much authority into these untested new entities. As a result, a deal had to be struck which allowed only Cuyahoga County to have such a county land bank. Senator Cates was in favor of the bill as written, but ultimately had to relent to the Cuyahoga County-only application of the bill. This was a victory for Cuyahoga County, but a temporary setback for the land banking movement in Ohio. This was especially so at a time when so many counties were struggling to find solutions to the real estate market collapse. Senator Cates encouraged us to view Cuyahoga County as the pilot land bank which if successful, other counties would demand the right to establish. His prediction would prove right. He remains a strong friend to the land banking movement for helping this bill pass the Ohio Senate.

When the bill reached the House, it was assigned to a committee and was considered a "pilot" project of the General Assembly applicable only to Cuyahoga County. Our sponsor in the House was then-Representative Matt Dolan (now State Senator Dolan). Representative Dolan quickly studied the bill to understand its depth and breadth. I knew he was seriously engaged. I was in a Columbus hotel room the night before the bill was to pass out of the House Committee. Questions had been raised by interest groups and other representatives. I was concerned because I had not spoken directly to Representative Dolan on the latest questions. I finally spoke to him in my hotel room that evening. I remember he was driving home from Toledo when he called me. We spoke for about an hour on the details of the bill and the questions that had been raised. After that call, I quickly took out my laptop and made some draft changes for submission the following day in anticipation of the hearing in the House. I made some changes to the governance sections and added some provisions that restricted county land banks from unduly competing with the OREIA constituency. I also prepared answers to anticipated questions Rep. Dolan said might arise at the hearing.

On the morning of the hearing our team was present and ready to testify in what we hoped would be a short hearing. Once again, last-minute drama emerged when one of the executives from Cleveland Mayor Jackson's office attended the committee hearing and lobbied members to delay the bill over issues of governance and board control of the new entity. The committee viewed this as last-minute distraction. After a few "side-bars" with Mayor Jackson's representative, we assured the representative that this entity would remain focused on the community development needs of *both* the county and city of Cleveland where much of the fallout occurred from the financial crisis.

Chris Warren, who was appointed by Mayor Jackson as the city's first appointee to the land bank board, was a fierce advocate for Cleveland (as we all were), and he made sure the city's interests were protected. He also understood better than most how powerful and useful a tool the county land bank could be to the city. His presence on our board brought deep knowledge that was needed at this start up stage.

After passage in the House Committee, Jim and I camped out that evening in the statehouse until the bill was put to a vote on the floor of the House that evening. Our presence at the statehouse to that point seemed like weeks. Jim and I were looking on from the House gallery when the bill was called, and it was surreal to be witnessing a vote being taken in the full House. The bill was passed by a resounding margin and on a hugely bipartisan basis. S.B. 353 was no longer a bill—it became an *act*. Representative Bill Batchelder, who was in the speaker's seat, stopped the proceedings and made a heartfelt tribute to Jim and our efforts. The entire House's attention was directed to where Jim and I were sitting, and they gave him an ovation. Jim had a tear in his eyes.

Within a year, then-Representative Peter Ujvagi passed a bill that opened up county land banking to counties with populations over 60,000, just as Senator Cates had predicted. Today, all counties (big and small) are authorized to form county land banks. As of this writing there are fifty-seven county land banks in Ohio.

NO LAND BANK	FEATURES & BENEFITS OF LAND BANKS
No strategic repository for bank REO, HUD, FNMA, FHLMC or GSE properties	Creates strategic repository
Disposition options constrained	Cycle of speculation terminated after redemption period expires
Encourages repeat cycles of speculation	Strategic disposition enhanced
Equity in property is depleted	Equity preserved for recapitalization
Inability to relocate willing owners	Can relocate existing owners
No system-wide protocols	Implement system-wide protocols with cities & REO's/GSE's
Lacks entrepreneurial capability	Entrepreneurial capabilities created
Unable to leverage existing equity	Existing equity can be leveraged
No capitalization mechanism	Capitalization mechanism created
Cumbersome bidding/RFP rules	Flexible bidding/RFP opportunities
Speculation	Buyers and rehabbers are vetted
No ability to work with lenders on loan & foreclosure counseling	Active counseling agreements with lenders & services

Chapter Six:
State and Federal Support

"A land bank with no money for demolition is like a new car with no gas: nice to look at but it doesn't take me anywhere."
—*Chuck Sammarone, mayor of Youngstown, Ohio, September 2011*

Jim Rokakis

The passage of Senate Bill 353 was great news for Cuyahoga County. The bill was signed into law December 2008, but it took six months of organizational work before the Cuyahoga County Land Reutilization Corporation (or the Cuyahoga Land Bank, for short) was operational. As county treasurer, I was one of the three initial incorporators, and served as the chairman of the board. We opened our doors on June 1, 2009.

The challenges of launching a county land bank were many: no one had ever organized anything like this before in Ohio. We had no rules or regulations governing our conduct. We knew that the new land bank bill had a mechanism that would provide a stream of income as we moved forward with hiring. But first, we had to decide what positions and functions were necessary. Gus Frangos immediately hired a chief operating officer— Bill Whitney, a veteran of the community development movement in Cleveland—and a chief financial officer shortly thereafter. He also understood the importance of data and recognized the genius of the Northeast Ohio Community and Neighborhood Data for Organizing (NEOCANDO) at Case Western Reserve University. NEOCANDO's property data collection systems at Case, under their Center on Urban Poverty and Community Development, were perhaps the finest in the country. Gus recognized that its director, Mike Schramm, was someone that he had to involve because data, good and reliable data, would help to drive decision-making. While Gus could not hire Schramm for another 18 months, he began to consult with Schramm almost immediately. Ultimately, Schramm would split his time between the land bank and NEOCANDO. In this way, Gus essentially brought NEOCANDO and all of its capabilities into the Cuyahoga Land Bank. The land bank secured office space on the corner of West Third and Lakeside, and began operations with a total of eight employees.

The first few months were spent completing the "office start-up" aspects of the operation—securing insurance, office space and lease, writing the employee manual, transactional forms, HR, and converting the points of property acquisition afforded by S.B. 353 from the theoretical to the practical. In the spring of 2010, HUD had put out request for proposals to apply for what was commonly known as Neighborhood Stabilization Program 2 (NSP-2) funds, which were essentially Troubled Asset Relief Program (TARP) funds aimed at addressing the foreclosure crisis. The funds would allow for demolition, foreclosure prevention, housing stabilization, and a host of other neighborhood stabilization interventions.

The Cleveland Housing Network was a powerful nonprofit in the area of affordable housing. Two of its leadership executives, Rob Curry and Kate Monter-Durban, met with Gus and me and advocated that the Cuyahoga Land Bank should apply for this grant, but as a consortium member consisting of Cuyahoga County, the Cuyahoga County Metropolitan Housing Authority, the City of Cleveland and the Cuyahoga Land Bank, with the Cuyahoga Land Bank as the lead consortium member. Chris Warren, in the mayor's cabinet, was in favor of this. After a lengthy application process, the Cuyahoga Land Bank was awarded $41 million, split among consortium members—this with not even a year under the land bank's belt. As a result, it would not be long before the land bank would need to hire additional employees to meet increasing demands put on the land bank by the emergence of the NSP-2 grant. Neighborhood organizations and cities all over the county were asking the newly formed county land bank to take distressed properties. The old idiom *be careful what you wish for* certainly applied here—almost immediately.

The rest of Ohio soon took notice of the Cuyahoga Land Bank's success. By the end of 2009, State Representative Peter Ujvagi from Toledo was working to amend Senate Bill 353 to allow additional counties to establish a land bank. His bill, House Bill 515, passed one year later to allow any counties over 60,000 in population to incorporate a land bank. The bill went to the floor with the population requirement set at 100,000, but was amended on the floor by State Representative Dennis Murray who wanted a land bank in his home county of Erie—so the amendment was introduced and passed on the floor.

Lucas County, through the efforts of County Treasurer Wade Kapszukiewicz (now mayor of Toledo), was the first county to take advantage of the bill. Immediately following Lucas County was Trumbull County, led by County Treasurer Sam Lamancusa and neighborhood activists at

Trumbull Neighborhood Partnership. I was thrilled to see them move so quickly as both treasurers were colleagues that were close to me, but my term as treasurer was winding down. The previous November, the effort to switch the county government to the executive form of government had passed, and my office would be abolished on the last day of December 2010. My days as an elected official were coming to an end.

During the process of lobbying influence makers in 2008 to garner support for S.B. 353, one of the people I met with was Rich Cochran, the CEO of Western Reserve Land Conservancy ("the Land Conservancy"). I was fortunate that these meetings had piqued his interest in land banks, and he extended an offer for me to join the Land Conservancy. Western Reserve Land Conservancy was recognized as one of the premier land conservation organizations in America, but had worked almost exclusively in rural and ex-urban areas. Yet Cochran envisioned expanded potential for their work through the land bank movement, with the powers that land banks possessed and the opportunities they presented for land conservation work in urban areas.

Rich and his team had recently completed a complex urban land acquisition project in Akron, Ohio. It was in a distressed area, dotted with junkyards, old industrial activity, brownfields, and residential areas that were troubled. To assemble only ten acres of land required the acquisition of some fifty parcels, many of which were vacant and abandoned properties. The project became known as Haley's Run. This took years of hard work. The Land Conservancy did not have the statutory powers of a county land bank, which would have provided several unique benefits including a fast track process for acquisition, environmental liability protections, and the ability to clear title problems by operation of law.

"When the Land Conservancy did a post mortem on the Haley's Run project, we drew an unwelcome conclusion: while this project was virtuous and even transformational for the community, it was not replicable, because to do several such projects would require 100 percent of the Land Conservancy's capacity; it would monopolize all of our resources to do even a few of these per year, as opposed to the fifty–seventy conventional conservation projects we were able to do each year," said Cochran of urban projects.

However, when Rich became aware of the special powers enjoyed by the new form of county land bank, he immediately realized that it would be beneficial for every county served by the Land Conservancy to have one, and that they would be powerful partners for similar organizations. Rich and several of his colleagues and trustees were also deeply committed to environmental and social justice, and felt that this would be an ideal way for them to seamlessly transition into more urban areas. Rich believed that in many legacy cities in Ohio there would soon be a glut of vacant land, some of which could be converted to green space in the form of urban farms, parks, and urban reforestation areas. These new green amenities would help to attract and retain a new generation of people to repopulate these Ohio cities, almost all of which had lost more than 50 percent of their residents since the 1960s. Rich envisioned a partnership between the county land banks and Western Reserve Land Conservancy in which the land banks would secure ownership of vacant land and the Land Conservancy would find ways to preserve and restore some of that land.

"At the Land Conservancy we believe that all living things, including people, naturally and subconsciously move away from things they perceive as toxic and towards things they perceive as nutrients," Cochran added. "The legacy cities of Ohio, such as Cleveland, were becoming more and more toxic which drove people to leave for 'greener pastures,' which caused urban sprawl … both exurban development and urban abandonment. The foreclosure crisis was the final straw. Thousands of newly vacant homes created a dystopic environment; the homes were frightening nearby residents, serial killers emerged in two Cleveland neighborhoods filled with vacant homes, and many became crash pads for drug users and other violent criminals. The Land Conservancy believed that if we could remove the toxicity of vacant and abandoned homes, and if we could endow these neighborhoods with restored green areas, then the healing would begin and it would last. What better way to stop urban sprawl than to improve the environmental conditions of our historic inner cities and first suburbs?"

Rich asked me to join his organization and establish an urban arm that came to be known as the Thriving Communities Institute (today, the Thriving Communities program). He realized that a land conservation organization could work in urban areas and was willing to take the leap of faith that such a move would require. It was not easy at first as some of the board members and staff expressed reservations about how a traditional land conservation organization would work in urban areas. Urban communities, in particular distressed urban communities, would pose significant challenges. Cities, and especially struggling neighborhoods, are often places where "sharp elbows" rule the day. Overwhelming problems coupled with limited resources make for very hard choices. But Cochran persevered and won his Board over. On March 1, 2011, I joined Western

Reserve Land Conservancy and learned quickly that its influence was such that the work that needed to be done could be accomplished more easily than by going it alone, without the support of a highly regarded organization and its influential board members. The Land Conservancy had deep and trusting relationships with elected and appointed officials across the entire political spectrum.

Originally, we had planned to work in the Land Conservancy's footprint, which was approximately fifteen Ohio counties extending from Erie County east to the Pennsylvania border, south to Mahoning County and back west again through counties like Portage, Summit, Stark, Medina, and Huron. Soon it became clear to all of us that our mission would expand into other areas. In fact, one of the first calls to our office requesting assistance came from Hamilton County (Cincinnati). It was well outside our footprint, but some of the strongest resistance to a land bank bill came from this county's state legislators—so we felt the need to establish a land bank there quickly—to prove to its detractors that it could work. All of Ohio was experiencing the deleterious effects of the foreclosure crisis, and in order to build an effective political platform we needed to both network and act in all corners of the State.

On one of my first visits to Mahoning County, Youngstown Mayor Chuck Sammarone asked me a blunt and direct question: "Do you have money for demolition in these land banks? Because if you can't help me get control of these vacant properties and tear them down, then the land bank is like a new car with no gas—it's nice to look at but it doesn't take me anywhere." The metaphor was powerful, and I heard that theme reiterated over and over as I travelled the state. "Yes," I would hear, "we are interested in a land bank, but we would be a whole lot more interested if we could find the resources to deal with this problem of blight." In the summer of 2013, we worked with graduate students from Cornell University, led by Isaac Robb, now a member of the Thriving Communities staff, to survey communities in Ohio to realistically estimate that blight. We had anecdotal evidence, but we struggled with data being sorely lacking in virtually every community we surveyed. All you needed to do was drive through the inner cities of Cleveland, Youngstown, Warren, Canton, Toledo, Dayton, and others to realize that the problem of blight was real—and at times overwhelming.

We learned early on that this issue was not just a big-city problem. We saw blight in small communities all over Ohio in Lima, Mansfield, Sydney, Wellston, Chillicothe, and many of the counties along the Ohio River—

towns, cities, and villages like Pomeroy, Middleport, and Portsmouth. No, this was not just a big city problem, it was an Ohio problem. Ohio saw so many of its factories and businesses leave, and saw much of its population go with it. We came to learn that when those businesses all left, they didn't take their factories—their physical plants—with them.

Because quality data was scarce, we settled on a methodology to determine vacancy that relied on a combination of factors, including postal vacancy data and abandonment around the state. We requested public condemnation records from building departments across the state and used various methods to try to determine the vacancy rate in communities where data-gathering was weak. We quickly arrived at a number of approximately 100,000 units that awaited demolition in Ohio. We knew from experience that the average demolition would cost approximately $10,000. So we had a billion-dollar problem, and no funds to address it, other than the DTAC funding that supported land bank staff and sporadic field maintenance, some renovations, and emergency demolitions in communities all over Ohio. For land banks to work most effectively, we needed serious dollars—not just DTAC funding. Enormous sums of money would be required to address this widespread problem.

We began to strategize how to find funding for blight removal in the summer of 2011. We looked at the state budget, which was strapped, and we didn't get a strong sense of commitment from the state government. While the problem of blight affected all types of communities, unfortunately, we understood from legislative leaders that they viewed this as an inner-city problem. In our experience, problems of the inner city did not have a lot of traction at the state capital in Columbus. They still don't—although that is changing as of this writing due to Governor DeWine's interest in the mission of blight removal. (DeWine is very familiar with the need, having supported a larger infusion of demolition capital from a national mortgage fraud settlement. His "Moving Ohio Forward" was a watershed moment for land banks and their development.)

We looked at federal dollars as another possibility. We were concerned because, while we had a sympathetic ear in the White House with President Barack Obama, Congress was divided and getting new dollars to address blight in Ohio was a longshot. I was working hard to raise awareness of the problem nationally. I wrote a piece in the *Washington Post* about the need to raise demolition dollars. We were in touch with Gretchen Morgenson, the *New York Times* business reporter, who did phenomenal national reporting on the foreclosure crisis between 2000 and 2010. We asked her to investigate the problem of vacant and abandoned properties, and she wrote a very powerful piece about the need to find legal settlement dollars. We had another great stroke of luck: in October 2011, I was approached by the television program *60 Minutes* to speak about the problem of blight in America. They talked to me and other Clevelanders for weeks, and decided to do an episode on blight and remediation efforts in Cleveland, Ohio. They sent a crew here in October 2011 and the episode—entitled "There Goes the Neighborhood"—ran December 18 of that year, directly after one of the most highly watched NFL games in CBS history, and was seen by millions of viewers.

Luck definitely played a role in the timing of the *60 Minutes* episode. Just a week before the episode ran, I paid a visit to the then-Attorney General of Ohio, Mike DeWine, and to the U.S. Treasury Department. Through the auspices of Western Reserve Land Conservancy and their lobbying team, we were able to get an audience with DeWine to discuss the impending "Robo-signing" settlement. The "Robo-signing" lawsuit was brought by fifty state Attorneys General against the five major banks for fraud in the filing of foreclosure actions around the country. We knew the lawsuit had been settled for $25 billion, and that a percentage, albeit a relatively small amount, would be set aside for state governments—in particular the Attorneys General—to allocate as they saw fit. The vast majority of the $25 billion went to borrowers who had been illegally foreclosed upon. Our argument to the attorney general was that the victims of the foreclosure crisis were not only those who lost their homes or those who had been foreclosed illegally, but the homeowners who were left in those neighborhoods—homeowners who paid their taxes on time and had taken care of their property. They played by the rules and had done nothing wrong. Unfortunately for most of them, this crisis had wiped out the majority of their home equity. We argued to Attorney General DeWine that they were also victims and that we needed a portion, if not all, of the "Robo-signing" dollars to deal with the problem of blight and abandonment. That Monday morning, he made no commitment, but he clearly understood the issue's gravity based on his questions and comments to us.

"You were very influential in that decision," DeWine told us years later, after he was sworn in as governor. "I think frankly, if it wasn't for you, we wouldn't have done it, because I think you were the advocate of that and made a case that this would have a real impact. So I think that's number one. Number two, I've learned in public office that sometimes you need to target a problem and then just go directly at the problem. We could have taken—we had $93 million. We took $75 million and put it into this project. We could have split it up fifty different ways. We could have done ten. But I wanted to be able to have a real impact in some area.

"[. . .] I knew, from travelling around the state and talking to mayors and county officials, commissioners, mayors, etc., that everybody had this problem. This was not something that was just in the cities. You know, we knew it was a big problem. For example, I lived in Miami Valley, we knew it was a big problem in Dayton. But really, you made the case that this is something that could be done that would have an impact on communities."

Attorney General DeWine responded almost immediately after our 2011 meeting. Within a week, he called and informed us that he would be committing $75 million of the $93 million that Ohio was awarded through the "Robo-signing" settlement. Additionally, he hired Thriving Communities to help roll out the program, which would provide these dollars to county land banks, if the county had one, or otherwise to a county through the county treasurer. The attorney general wanted to take his $75 million commitment for blight removal, and do even more by leveraging.

"So we took it from there, and said 'okay how are we going to do it?' And really, went through a number of different options, but decided that for the larger counties, you know, we would have a match requirement. And the whole idea is to make the money go further to get some buy-in from the local community. But we also knew that a county like Pike County—kind of hard to come up with a match. And so we came up with this kind of hybrid system" DeWine explained. "What we found is that the capacity in different counties were different—shouldn't shock us."

The attorney general's plan to leverage the settlement dollars made money available to every county in Ohio, based on foreclosure filings in that county, up to $500,000, as a grant. Anything above $500,000 had to be matched by the local county. Every single county that was eligible for a match took him up on the offer. As a result, $47 million additional dollars were raised by this leveraging requirement. The program was simple—all the county had to do was demonstrate that the property had been taken down, provide the proper documentation and evidence of the expense, and the state would reimburse the county. When the funds ran out and the program was shut down, in March 2015, over $119 million had been spent and over 14,600 abandoned structures had been removed. Local government officials throughout Ohio still talk about this as being the best program they were ever involved with, because of its simplicity and prompt reimbursements.

The day after we saw the attorney general, we traveled to the U.S. Treasury Department for a meeting set up by Ohio Congresswoman Marcy Kaptur where, as luck would have it, we had a great contact. Don Graves, one of the assistant undersecretaries of the treasury, was a classmate of Rich Cochran's at University School, a private boys school in Northeast Ohio. Graves had served in numerous roles in the Obama administration, but had moved to the Department of the Treasury where his actual title was Deputy Assistant Secretary for Small Business, Community Development Policy. We had a warm reception there. Treasury, because of the role assigned them by the Congress to save the American banking system, was in a unique position to help.

Our argument to Treasury was simple: there were thousands and thousands of vacant and abandoned properties in cities like Cleveland, Toledo, Youngstown, and other communities all over America. We knew, based on our experiences that homebuyers were walking away from their mortgages in record numbers. And it made good economic sense: in a "normal" mortgage market when homebuyers put 20 percent down on the sale of the property, values would have to plummet more than 20 percent before buyers would consider leaving the property to "cut their losses." But, when homebuyers were able to buy a property with little or no money down, and property values began to decline, they had little incentive to stay. One study, in noting this trend said, "Such behavior, where not precipitated by willful fraud, shows that American homebuyers supposedly duped by their lenders aren't so dumb. They're perfectly capable of acting rationally without political interference." By the time we visited the Treasury, because of the collapse of Fannie Mae, the federal government was backstopping nine out of ten mortgages through the Treasury Department. We argued before Treasury that if they helped us demolish vacant and abandoned properties at the cost of about $10,000 per home, there would be a stronger likelihood that the neighbors who lived on those blocks would stay in their homes, because they would have more confidence in that neighborhood's ability to hold its value. All it took was one discouraged neighbor to leave a property, and the federal government would have to backstop the mortgage for as much as $100,000 or $150,000—or more. We argued that they were far better off by helping us raze vacant and abandoned properties. That would be the best way to prevent foreclosures, and to prevent the government from having to back more failed mortgages.

At the end of that meeting, we were approached by a high-ranking Treasury official who asked to speak to us outside of the meeting.

David Dworkin was a manager of the Capital Magnet Fund at the U.S. Community Development Financial Institutions (CDFI) at that time, although he moved to Treasury as a policy advisor the following month. He said that he was in complete agreement with us and that he knew that vacant properties were a crushing problem—especially in the Midwest. As a native Detroiter he knew better than most how the problem of vacant and abandoned properties was crippling cities and preventing these communities from moving forward. He promised us that he would work with us towards a solution, and intimated that he knew where there might be dollars to assist us in our efforts.

Within a week of our first meeting Dworkin authored a memo to Graves talking about the need for demolition funding, how vacant homes in distressed communities were being stripped quickly and losing almost all of their value and seriously impacting values on surrounding residential properties. The memo concluded that funding for demolition given the political realities in Washington—a Congress that denied President Obama on almost every new initiative—was going to be extremely difficult.

But Dworkin and Graves persisted. They turned their attention to a fund called the Hardest Hit Fund (HHF). The program was set up in 2008 when TARP was created to prevent the banking system from collapsing under the weight of the millions of failed mortgages. One way of making this bank bailout bill more palatable for Congress was to create a program within TARP that would also aid homeowners facing foreclosure. This assistance came in the form of additional loans that would assist homeowners with cash to make good on their past due mortgage payments and move that new debt to the back end of the mortgage. The Hardest Hit Fund was not a national program but targeted to eighteen states (along with the District of Columbia) that were most directly impacted by the foreclosure crisis. Fortunately for our efforts, Ohio was one of them.

Throughout the early part of 2012, Dworkin and Graves continued to meet with Kaptur and had discussions with Ohio Senator Sherrod Brown as well about where funds could be found that would assist demolition efforts in Ohio. It was clear to policy makers at Treasury that the program would either be a national program or be part of an existing effort that had a focus larger than one or two states. The idea of reprogramming HHF dollars for demolition gained increased favor in Treasury since so many of the eighteen states in the program, most notably Ohio, Michigan, and Indiana, were so severely afflicted with vacant properties

"Don and I were thinking outside the box," said Dworkin. "Typically, issues like this flow in the HUD policy lane, but they had no money. Treasury had the money to help with this problem, but we had to convince people higher up in Treasury that we could do this. We needed them to think outside the box as well."

Don Graves was the sole political appointee in Treasury whose job was to focus in on issues related to "Main Street.'" "Most of the rest of Treasury was focused on things like macroeconomic policy, international finance, capital markets, issues related to social security payments, and government finance, things like that," he said. "Because my role was focused on small business, housing, and community and economic development issues, I was focused on what was going on with 'Main Streets' across the country—what people dealt with in their daily lives. [Your] request came at the perfect time […] we had fairly recently implemented a program called the Hardest Hit Fund."

Graves went on to explain the purpose of the program; "it was to stabilize housing markets, get equity back in homes again, get the market working the way that it should. The only way to do that in many of the Hardest Hit Fund communities was if we were actually able to go in and target those properties that were bringing down the rest of the neighborhood properties, and those properties were ones that couldn't be rehabbed, it would just cost too much, and it made a whole lot more sense as a result then to demolish homes."

The repurposing of Hardest Hit Fund dollars from mortgage foreclosure relief became the focus of Treasury as the best source of available funds that could be used for demolition. The one significant legal hurdle that had to be overcome was that the use of these funds had to be proven to prevent foreclosures. Many studies talked about how vacant properties destabilized neighborhoods and reduced property values of surrounding properties, but a more definitive study focused more narrowly on the relationship between demolition and foreclosures would have to be undertaken.

Graves and Dworkin, and others at Treasury including Benson Roberts, realized that in order for Treasury to move on the reallocation there would have to be a larger public meeting where higher ups at Treasury, including Michael Stegman, would not only be given the chance to buy in to this concept, but also to accept the fact that these funds were not coming back to the Treasury and, unlike mortgage foreclosure prevention loans, this principal would be forgiven. Stegman was a former professor of public policy at Duke who was serving as counselor to the secretary of the treasury for housing finance policy.

This interagency meeting, titled "Residential Property Vacancy and Abandonment," was convened in Treasury on September 24. There were multiple panels and breakout sessions around the impact of vacancy and potential strategies to deal with the vacancy problem. I was on a panel with Nigel Griswold, an econometrician from Michigan who had served as a research fellow with the Center for Community Progress and had done work for Dan Kildee and his land bank in Genesee County, Michigan. Griswold impressed them with his work and ended up spending considerable time that afternoon with Stegman discussing how a study could be done that would show the connection between demolition and foreclosure prevention.

At the conclusion of that meeting on September 24, we were given a task: Stegman told us that we needed to conduct a study that demonstrated a direct relationship between demolition and how demolition could lower the foreclosure rate.

The study was expensive. The Thriving Communities program had to raise over $140,000, which we obtained through the contributions of fourteen land banks in Ohio. Griswold began his work in November 2012, and his efforts did not go unnoticed. Our office received a call from Wayne Ting in the White House Office of Economic Policy in December 2012 requesting immediate access to the data that Griswold was compiling and analyzing. We told them the study was months away from being completed, but the White House asked for the data in current time. So as Nigel was conducting his study, he was sending his data to the White House advisers. On June 3, 2013, we received a call from the White House telling us that although the study was not complete, they had seen enough data to convince them that they could justify allowing the Hardest Hit Fund money to be used for demolition. We were ecstatic. The completed study, entitled "Estimating the Effect of Demolishing Distressed Structures in Cleveland, Ohio. 2009–2013: Impacts on Real Estate Equity and Mortgage-Foreclosure," was not released until the fall of that year.

The first $80 million in Ohio was made available immediately. Due to the manner in which the federal regulations were written and how properties had to be held, only counties with a county land bank were eligible to receive the dollars. Within days, we were receiving calls from all over Ohio requesting information on how to start a county land bank. When that ruling was made, there were twenty-one land banks. Within the year, the number had doubled, and continued to increase. As of the writing of this book, there are fifty-seven land banks in Ohio.

As it turns out, it was providential that the Cuyahoga Land Bank was the first land bank to be up and operating. It had the expertise of the original S.B. 353 draft writer—Gus Frangos—who had already developed the needed forms, templates, practice guidelines and knowledge of the interplay with county government. This allowed a healthy amount of tutoring in the early days, along with a "playbook" that Gus developed for all land banks, refined and made available by Thriving Communities.

Because the Hardest Hit Fund program was housed in the Ohio Housing Finance Agency (OHFA), Treasury decided the demolition funds would be administered there as well. It wasn't a perfect fit but OHFA stepped up and quickly set up a program that would administer these funds. The funds were sucked up quickly by the older, more established land banks, but it didn't take long for newer land banks to get up to speed on how to acquire abandoned properties and apply to OHFA for funding. Smaller counties like Allen, Ashtabula, Jefferson, Lawrence, Mahoning, and Trumbull successfully applied for and collectively received tens of millions of dollars to remove vacant and abandoned homes in their counties.

Cuyahoga County and the City of Cleveland have taken additional extraordinary measures to deal with vacant and abandoned properties. The City of Cleveland has committed $94 million dollars since 2006 to deal with vacant and abandoned properties. This commitment has resulted in 11,000 structures being demolished—primarily residential but also commercial and industrial structures. Cleveland has steadfastly devoted more resources to the issue of blight reduction than any other community in the state of Ohio.

But additional steps were taken by Cuyahoga County government in the fall of 2013. That year, at the State of the County address, County Executive Ed Fitzgerald made a $50 million commitment for blight removal in Cuyahoga County. This came on the heels of a study done by Robin Thomas, the land bank program director at Western Reserve Land Conservancy, and a former *Plain Dealer* reporter named Mark Gillespie. The study, entitled "The Cost of Vacancy—Everybody Pays" demonstrated that the loss of values and property tax collections in Cleveland and its inner-ring suburbs had created a shift in tax collections totaling $48 million. The study demonstrated that there were four countywide levies—the Cuyahoga Community College, the Port Authority, the Metroparks, and the Health and Human Services Levy—that were collected from every community in Cuyahoga County. When property values plummeted in distressed communities it did nothing more than shift the tax burden to other more stable communities throughout the county. This $48 million shift was proof that while you could live in a comfortable suburban neighborhood and say that vacant properties were not your problem, they in fact were, and it resulted in higher property tax payments for everybody else.

By the end of 2019, nearly 40,000 structures had been demolished in Ohio through the Moving Ohio Forward Program, Hardest Hit Fund dollars, and the commitments from Cuyahoga County government.

Chapter Seven:
The Cuyahoga Land Bank

"Taking all CCRLC expenditures and measurable programmatic activity
into account, research confirms a total estimated economic impact of
$1.43 billion in Cuyahoga County since inception in 2009."
—*Nigel Griswold, CEO of Dynamo Metrics, June 2019*

Gus Frangos

The Cuyahoga Land Bank opened its doors on June 1, 2009. Our
governance at that time consisted of then-County Treasurer board chairman
Jim Rokakis and former commissioners Peter Lawson Jones and Jimmy
Dimora. Those three board members served by virtue of statute (1724.02).
Together, they appointed the balance of our board consisting of various
officials throughout the county. They appointed me as the first president of
the first county land bank in the state of Ohio.

In anticipation of this appointment, I began interviewing and
assembling a team that I thought would be dedicated and passionate about
this new mission, as well as possessing the necessary expertise to launch
this "land bank on steroids." At our first staff meeting— consisting of all
of eight people—I told these eight individuals that they were destined to
become the "A-Team" of county land banking throughout the country.
It was a very big—and scary—vision that I was casting considering that
we were sitting in a circle of chairs with no other furniture and no office
equipment to speak of.

Knowing that we would be transacting extensively in real estate, I
brought together all of the legal forms developed throughout my thirty
years of law practice that I thought might have some relevancy to our work.
To this day, most of these forms have been adapted and modified by the
excellent staff charged with implementing the numerous transactions we
deal with.

We operated, and continue to operate, under two axioms: (1) hurdles
are a good thing because hurdles can be overcome; and (2) we avoid
"thinking out of the box." Instead, maximum creativity to experiment
would be to work "without reference" to any boxes at all.

Milestones: Research and Collaboration

With the influx of demolition dollars coming from the federal government's NSP-2 Program, followed by then-Attorney General Mike DeWine's Moving Ohio Forward Program and later supplemented by Cuyahoga County's Demolition Program, and finally OHFA's Neighborhood Initiative Program (NIP), the challenge to be strategic and impactful was paramount. At the time, board of revision tax foreclosures were in full swing and the BOR process was embraced by all county agencies touching upon tax foreclosure. Because there were tens of thousands of vacant and abandoned properties needing tax foreclosure, the challenge was to target properties in a way that would make the most impact seeing as the county could only appropriate enough dollars to foreclose on roughly 3,000 properties per year.

In those early days, Michael Schramm worked for Case Western Reserve's NEOCANDO Center, traditionally known as the Poverty Center. The center accumulated data on social trends and later real estate trends. This included tracking of properties and the integration of public data bases including the offices of the county treasurer, auditor, clerk of courts, and U.S. Postal Service among others. To this day, this tool undergirds all of the research systems employed by the Cuyahoga Land Bank. It was imperative to hire Mike and secure his access to NEOCANDO, which I did.

Michael Schramm developed systems to enhance the capabilities of NEOCANDO so that very early on we were able to turn the tax foreclosure process from a random collection practice to a highly strategic community development tool. Using the U.S. Postal Service database, for example, we were able to make high-level assessments of which properties were vacant and abandoned throughout the county. This was supplemented by building and housing data from the various municipalities, as well as on-the-ground input from community development corporations (CDCs) based on observation. Local government planning departments, park districts, CDC target areas, and economic development assemblages served as the strategic filters to which parcels would be directed for tax foreclosure.

Mike further developed a spatial analysis tool that would allow us to identify adjacencies that would promote strategic redevelopment and land assemblages. An excellent example of this would be the assembly of the lots forming what would become the Fisher House. This resulted in a $17 million thirty-three-unit extended-stay housing complex for the families of combat-injured veterans who were confined to the Cleveland VA hospital. This assemblage, only one block from the VA hospital, took several years, several demolitions, and coordination with the Office of Veterans Affairs. (More on Fisher House later.)

In the early days, we spent much time meeting with our treasurer, prosecutor and local CDCs making sure that everyone cooperated in this endeavor. By 2011, the Cuyahoga Land Bank and all of the county agencies developed a protocol that allowed the Cuyahoga Land Bank to serve as the clearing house for referring "batches" of abandoned delinquent properties to the county treasurer for tax foreclosure as well as referrals known as "one-offs." Batches consisted of the strategic data-driven referrals while "one-offs" consisted of tax foreclosures submitted by local non-profits, CDCs and businesses seeking to acquire abandoned land. Inasmuch as an excellent working relationship developed early with the county prosecutor and treasurer, this clearing house function would be performed by the Cuyahoga Land Bank, which was more adept at tracking the trajectories of each individual batched or on-off property. Stakeholders thus submitted tax-foreclosure-eligible properties to the Cuyahoga Land Bank. We curated each request to make sure that it was indeed tax foreclosure eligible, that there were no bankruptcies, payment plans, or other impediments to foreclosure. By 2012, this process turned out to be one of the most efficient inter-agency processes, and it persists to this day.

Deed-in-Escrow

One of the early most troublesome problems for cities, CDCs, and our land bank was how to enforce quality and expeditious renovations of properties that were in our inventory. While we needed to move these properties, we could not do so unless the property was disposed of to responsible rehabbers. In the early days, flipping of vacant and abandoned properties was rampant and literally terrorizing whole neighborhoods. By 2011, we were bringing in roughly 100 properties per month, 35 percent of which could be renovated. The remaining 65 percent required demolition because the house was beyond renovation.

For those properties suitable for renovation, a major question was how to make sure that once we conveyed a property to a renovator, that the property would in fact get renovated according to code as opposed to falling back into the cycle of abandonment and tax delinquency. Conventional practice is to place deed restrictions and deed reverters onto deeded properties. Reverters are ineffective in that if a renovator did not meet the needed requirements to renovate a home, the property was already conveyed and would require litigation to enforce the reverter. Instead, we developed what is known as the Deed-in-Escrow program. This was a simple yet unique practice of marketing our properties to renovators, letting them fully inspect the property beforehand, and agreeing to a pre-prepared work specification prepared by the land bank. The specifications conformed to a "code plus" standard which simply means that the specification is designed to require a code compliant renovation plus additional safety features unique to the particular property. Professional software and specification writers prepared each specification by visiting each home. It cost about $150 per specification. An owner or renovator wishing to acquire the property needed to first look at the specification which was posted on our website with the property listing. Portions of the specification could be negotiated if reasonable. Our programs department would conduct a soft underwriting which required the renovator or would-be homeowner to identify a modicum of resources commensurate with the amount of work identified in the specification.

Once these things were accomplished, we would "eye" the prospective purchaser. The "EYE" examination is a vetting system which seeks to determine if the purchaser or his company is currently tax delinquent on existing owned properties, has existing code violations, or is in a chain of known flippers or bad actors. We'd then check public databases, including those of the Ohio Secretary of State, building department records of the particular municipality, and auditor and treasurer tax records. The intent here is to try to make responsible dispositions to qualified rehabbers.

Once this function was completed, we would turn the keys over to the would-be renovator, turn on the lights and give them anywhere between three to six months to complete the renovation. The key to the program is that the deed is held in escrow until the work specification is completed. In order to measure progress, an inspection would occur every thirty days. The renovator and inspector relationship requires only a check-off system on each item of the specification in order to have the deed transferred. In each case, a price for the property would be negotiated considering market conditions in the particular neighborhood, and the extent of needed renovation. In this way, if the property did not get renovated according to specification, the deed would not be conveyed. This was a much easier and self-executing enforcement mechanism to assure a quality renovation than deed restrictions or the deed reverter technique. Just as important, this process weeds out those trying to acquire and flip our properties without rehabbing them.

As of this writing, more than 1,900 properties have been renovated either internally or through the deed-in-escrow program. Less than ten properties have proven unsuccessful requiring us to take the property back. Renovators like the program because it offers transparency and reliability. Renovators can thoroughly inspect a property beforehand, evaluate the specification, and if the specification is performed, they will receive a deed.

"Showing" and Marketing Properties

Early on, a practical hurdle had to do with how we effectively market and show the properties for sale. With more than 100 properties flooding into our inventory monthly, this was a significant issue. Initially, we started by retaining realtors. Many problems were confronted. First, because many of these properties sold from anywhere between $5,000 and $10,000, it was not worth a realtor's time to market these properties unless we agreed to a fixed commission of a few thousand dollars if the property sold. Second, because the deed would not be transferred to the buyer until the renovation was completed, it was extremely cumbersome for a realtor to keep track of the progress of the work and to communicate specification requirements. Realtors simply prefer to list a property, show it, and then sell it. Third, paying a realtor a few thousand dollars for a property that we were selling for $5,000 did not yield sufficient income to compensate us for all of the curating, holding, and field servicing of these properties while in our inventory.

By this time, we had more interest in our properties than we could service in a traditional realtor setting. As the saying goes, necessity is the mother of invention. We established an on-line system of "showing" properties using "showers." In other words, once a property was placed on our website for sale, if buyers wanted to see the property, they would click a link indicating their interest. That link would automatically send an email to a grouping of four to six "showers" who were pre-approved by the Cuyahoga Land Bank's programs department. The first shower to respond to the interested buyer would be assigned to that showing. That shower would correspond directly with the buyer and arrange for a time that both of them could meet at the site. The shower merely opened the door for the buyer and accompanied the buyer through the inspection. Once the buyer's inspection was concluded, the shower would re-secure the property. If the buyer desired to take it to the next step, at that point he or she would work directly with land bank staff in the deed-in-escrow process. Each shower would be paid approximately $50 per showing. Hence, even if a property were shown ten times, that would still cost less than a traditional commission. Moreover, it brought buyers directly into the deed-in-escrow process managed by our staff. This process was crucial in the marketing of our properties, because we simply could not dedicate internal staff to run out and show hundreds of properties every time a buyer expressed an interest. In any given month, hundreds of inquiries were made requiring properties to be shown. This process allowed it all to happen electronically between the shower and the prospective purchaser.

HUD and FNMA

Despite our good intentions and attempts at performing a triage and assessment on all properties coming into our inventory through BOR tax foreclosure, an unintended but very destabilizing practice was occurring in our county. Because the Federal National Mortgage Association (FNMA) and the Department of Housing and Urban Development (HUD) had insured many of the loans that had defaulted, these agencies found themselves now holding hundreds of thousands of properties throughout the country and thousands in Cuyahoga County, the majority vacant and abandoned. Thinking that they were being good fiduciaries and protecting the taxpayer, these agencies were selling these properties for pennies on the dollar. Buyers were buying the properties in bulk without even taking the keys or inspecting the homes. They simply were wholesaling, distributing, and retailing properties in a massive flipping operation. It was the equivalent in trafficking in junk bonds. FNMA and HUD felt that to limit their losses it would be good to sell these properties for any amount and thereby recover dollars. This would also avoid the large field maintenance and transaction costs associated with holding the properties.

We spoke to both of these agencies and asked them if they would stop this practice. City of Cleveland officials were already pushing them as well. To their credit HUD and FNMA agreed to transfer all properties with a value of $25,000 and under directly to the Cuyahoga Land Bank. After much negotiation and cooperation between the Cuyahoga Land Bank, the City of Cleveland and these two agencies, a deal was struck with both of them to transfer their low-value assets to the Cuyahoga Land Bank instead of indiscriminately selling to anyone, often sight unseen. In the case of properties requiring demolition, FNMA would pay for a portion of the demolition cost; in the case of HUD, there would be no reimbursement for demolition, but transfers would occur for a purchase price of $100. By doing this, irresponsible transactions on the open market regarding these distressed properties eventually stopped. This in turn blunted the very destabilizing effect on comparable values from HUD and FNMA selling properties for pennies on the dollar. At that time, the Cuyahoga Land Bank was the first non-profit agency to have such "pooling" arrangements with FNMA and HUD.

Between 35 percent and 40 percent of the properties coming to the Cuyahoga Land Bank from these agencies were suitable for renovation either internally by the land bank itself or through the deed-in-escrow process. Based on the ten-year economic impact study completed by Dynamo Metrics and announced at Cleveland State University in June 2019, these efforts had an overall economic impact of $1.43 billion from 2010 to 2019! This would include tax base stabilization, economic activity associated with renovations, tax collection, job creation, and actual dollars expended.

Although the HUD acquisition numbers have decreased as of 2019, the Cuyahoga Land Bank continues to enjoy a solid relationship with HUD and maintains the pooling arrangement. In the early days, these pooling arrangements were bringing in close to sixty to seventy properties per month. Today, the land bank does not have a pooling arrangement with FNMA. Today our HUD acquisitions range from five to ten properties monthly due to improved market conditions. We cannot thank HUD enough for its partnership. It has made a tremendous difference in our housing stabilization efforts throughout the county.

Social Service and Faith-Based Partners

In the early days, there were some properties that had good bones and were located in areas where the market had not totally collapsed. Nevertheless, we could not even give these homes away. There was such a surplus of inventory and hesitancy to get into real estate that we were confronted with an ever-increasing inventory without the ability to sell properties to responsible homebuyers or qualified investors. Of course, the initial obvious reason was that many of these homes could not turn a profit even after a quality renovation. There were instances, for example, where a $20,000 renovation would barely produce that same amount upon resale. Hence, it was a simple business decision not to invest in these homes. This applied to CDCs as well, since they typically would seek buyers who could afford to pay the renovation costs and make a reasonable return on investment. Would-be owner occupants displayed the same reluctance—they did not want to spend money on a home renovation when the home would end up being valued less than the modest renovation costs.

How were we to try to market these homes that otherwise were in decent shape? A very potent and untapped constituency consisted of the faith-based community as well as several social service agencies providing wraparound services to "special populations." Special populations would include veterans, congregate living for those recovered from addiction, re-entry clientele, persons with handicaps, senior citizens, refugees, and adults aging out of foster care. Although the Cuyahoga Land Bank itself is not a provider of social services, amongst the menu of needed wraparound services (regardless of the special population group), housing is a universal wraparound need. In other words, whatever special population group a person was in, and whatever services they needed, one service common to all of these individuals was the need for housing. As a result, we embarked upon a mission to enlist as many of these agencies that were willing to take our surplus homes for little or no cost so that they could in turn, deploy their existing base of philanthropy to renovate and populate these homes for properly vetted clientele. These stakeholder institutions were not so interested in investing for a "profit" as they were mission-minded and wanting to provide safe, clean and affordable housing for their clients.

This was one of the greatest initiatives of the Cuyahoga Land Bank in terms of deepening its roots in the community. By this point, the Cuyahoga Land Bank had developed a good reputation for doing brick and mortar work and collaborating with municipalities, CDCs, renovators, and contractors. However, teaming up with organizations like the City Mission, Bessie's Angels, Building Hope in the City, Women of Hope, and others put the word out that the Cuyahoga Land Bank not only addresses brick and mortar issues but desires also to partner with those agencies providing direct wraparound services to special populations. As of the end of 2019, the Cuyahoga Land Bank has worked with more than forty organizations and faith-based institutions. These organizations in some cases have done one project, while others, such as Habitat for Humanity, have done over fifty homes.

From Demolition to Development

We like to say that we "wrote the book" on demolition practice for land banks. Until the end of 2018, Cheryl Stephens was the Director of Acquisition, Disposition and Development for the Cuyahoga Land Bank until she went on to become the director of the East Akron Neighborhood Development Corporation. Cheryl, in fact, literally did write the book on demolition. She not only created a handbook, *The A to Z of Demolition Practice*, but she designed a system of best practices which promoted integrity in the procurement process. Demolition involves many aspects.

Once acquired, a property must initially be assessed; then surveyed for asbestos; then properly remediated and asbestos disposed of all in compliance with regulatory practice. Next, a demolition specification must be created; then competitive bids and vendors procured; then bid awards; then the site must be monitored for quality control, filling of the hole, and proper seeding and grating; followed ultimately by payment. If there was ever a need for perfection and high standards, demolition practice is where it is especially required. Cheryl came closer than anyone I know to meeting that standard. It must be remembered that more than 100 properties a month were streaming into our inventory which her staff had to assess. After this initial property assessment (internal and exterior) between 30 percent and 40 percent of those properties were being referred by her department to our director of programs, Dennis Roberts, who was responsible for further evaluating properties for our in-house renovation program or the deed-in-escrow program.

Dennis managed the disposition of all properties that were candidates for renovation. His operation developed an electronic system that placed the code compliance specifications onto our website along with each posted property, and managed the showing and ultimate disposition of these properties. It must be remembered that because the deed-in-escrow program did not result in an immediate transfer of title, Dennis developed a system of quality control monitoring every thirty days until the renovation was complete. Dennis and Cheryl did a remarkable job implementing the various programs of the Cuyahoga Land Bank, and have spoken at local and national conferences concerning best practices.

The important point to make is that while we were spending tens of millions of dollars in blight removal demolition, the Cuyahoga Land Bank was still the big gorilla when it came to facilitating home renovations. While many people viewed us as a demolition machine, we were the largest facilitator of renovated homes in the ten years since our inception.

Inasmuch as we were heavily engaged in home renovation, this was our entry into our current phase of land banking. Our focus beginning in 2020 is on housing development, new construction, and the role we can play in economic development based on the unique statutory tools afforded to county land banks. Although we will continue to do demolition and deed-in-escrow, we will have a greater role in housing and economic development. It is a natural transition.

Notable Project Milestones

As of December 2019, the Cuyahoga Land Bank has facilitated the renovation of just over 1,900 homes. As of that time, we have demolished more than 9,000 blighted and abandoned structures. Because of the powers and enablements authorized by the state legislature, land banks have been able to serve as great drivers of economic development projects. Indeed, land banks can purchase, sell, develop, joint venture, and essentially do everything that a private enterprise can do so long as the land bank adheres to its county-given plan. The thing that makes land banks such a potent tool is their ability to be much more nimble and able to execute transactions more quickly than government. Over the past ten years, hundreds of small business enhancement projects were facilitated for such things as parking, blight clearance, redevelopment, and expansion. Some of the larger and more notable success stories directly related to the powers of county land banks are listed below as examples.

North Randall Mall

This mall was the largest mall in the country at the time it opened. For over 15 years, it remained closed and abandoned, with millions of dollars of tax delinquencies. The Cuyahoga Land Bank helped assemble several of the parcels in this mall, which helped a developer to demolish and repurpose the entire site into a $171 million Amazon Fulfillment center, creating more than 2,500 jobs. North Randall Village Mayor David Smith said that the mall would never had been developed without the Cuyahoga Land Bank. New employees of the Amazon facility bought homes in neighboring Maple Heights, according to Maple Heights Mayor Annette Blackwell.

HGR Industries

This was a solid business tenant leasing its facility on a sixty-acre site containing other tenants with numerous jobs on the line. The owner of this site had allowed the property to become delinquent and ultimately abandoned portions of it. In order to preserve the property for all of the tenants, the property was ultimately assembled by the Cuyahoga Land Bank and resold back to the tenants, who completed a $12 million development including a new business with support from JobsOhio.

Greater Cleveland Fisher House

In 2015, when Greater Cleveland Fisher House president Tom Sweeney walked into our offices unannounced, asking that we help find some land for a Fisher House around the Louis Stokes Veterans' Hospital in Cleveland, we didn't even know what a Fisher House was. Fisher House is an organization that assembles and develops land and buildings around veterans' hospitals to provide extended-stay housing for families with hospitalized combat-disabled and -injured veterans. After conducting a thorough adjacency analysis around the Cleveland VA hospital, we identified a roughly two-acre site with parcels owned by our land bank, the City of Cleveland, and Famicos Development Corporation. Additional parcels needed to be assembled through tax foreclosure, while one was acquired by a tax lien certificate donation and another by direct purchase. Once assembled, all the parcels were consolidated into one parcel and conveyed to the U.S. Veterans Affairs Department to make way for the national Fisher House Foundation's development. In 2018, a ribbon cutting occurred for the two new Greater Cleveland Fisher Houses consisting of thirty-three units of luxury extended-stay housing. This was an especially rewarding project because up to this point families coming from out-of-town—and in many cases out-of-state—were required to secure hotel rooms that often were either unavailable or very expensive. There was no better way for the Cuyahoga Land Bank to honor our veterans than to help assemble these parcels.

Heinen's Expansion

Heinen's Groceries, a longtime big-box grocery chain and anchor head-quartered in Warrensville Heights, was considering moving to another city due to an urgent need to expand its facilities. But Mayor Brad Sellers pointed out the existence of a vacant and abandoned adjacent facility that was significantly tax delinquent that he convinced Heinen's to expand into if we could assemble the land. The abandoned building was eventually acquired and demolished by the Cuyahoga Land Bank, which resulted in a $9 million expansion of its Heinen's headquarters and distribution facilities.

YMCA Housing First

A long-closed and dilapidated YMCA building and adjacent abandoned commercial facility were acquired and demolished by the Cuyahoga Land Bank, which allowed the Housing First developer to secure tax credits resulting in a $13.9 million redevelopment consisting of seventy-one affordable housing units.

Many of the larger private economic development projects facilitated through the Cuyahoga Land Bank's services are included in Appendix 6 of its June 2019 *Cuyahoga Land Bank: 10-year Economic Impact Analysis.*

Policy and Legislation

One of the hallmarks of S.B. 353, which was passed in 2008 and became law in April 2009, was that it all turned out to be remarkably functional from an operational standpoint. In other words, legislation of this scope almost always has some glitches or some things that impede implementation that could not be anticipated. Once the Cuyahoga Land Bank began operating, followed by the authorization of all the other land banks throughout the State, many legislative enhancements were identified that helped make land bank operations even more efficient, even more transactional, and more impactful.

The Cuyahoga Land Bank has been instrumental in several additional modifications to various statutes designed to facilitate the efficient operations and transactions of county land banks. Today, the Cuyahoga Land Bank continues to be looked at as the policy leader throughout the state for engaging with the General Assembly and securing much needed community development and land bank legislation. This would not be possible without a very collaborative relationship between our county fiscal office, treasurer, county council, Clerk of Courts, Board of Revision, prosecutor, and sheriff's offices, not to mention our land bank partners throughout the state and statewide associations. It is to the great credit of these agencies that we have been able to accomplish so much in the areas of legislative reforms.

Chapter Eight:
County Land Banks

As reported by Dan McGraw and Jim Rokakis

Athens County Land Bank

As one drives into the southeast part of Ohio, the rolling hills become prettier and more Appalachian, and the expansive state parks and outdoor activities increase in popularity as tourist destinations. Athens County sits right in the heart of it.

A large university with a huge economic footprint, a historic coal mining and timber industry, farming that dates back 200 years, and a regional music center have made Athens County quite unique. But presently, the county is experiencing a period of economic transition, creating needs that the Athens County Land Bank serves to meet.

The land bank is fairly new, having been created in January 2018. The needs of the county are unique compared to most of those faced by Ohio county land banks; they tend not to be concentrated in high population areas like the city of Athens, but rather in some of the outlying smaller towns that are experiencing more transition.

"What we are finding is that areas like Glouster, Trimble Township, Nelsonville, and other places in the northwest part of the county are undergoing transitional needs, as the coal mining industry has largely left and the housing issues need to be addressed," said Athens County Treasurer and land bank board chair Ric Wasserman.

"The key part of the housing issue we are working on is that we are finding more and more twenty-five to thirty-four-year-olds are looking for to either open different types of businesses or are employed at the university, and want to find places to do so in the unique places we have in this county outside of Athens itself," he observed.

What makes this part of the land bank equation somewhat different is that the Athens County Land Bank is not doing much work—for now anyway—in the city of Athens. This is because the housing market for Ohio University is as stable as any college housing market can be, and the city zoning and code enforcement office, as well as the county treasurer's office, keep a keen eye on the housing stock in that community.

"It is not that there are no tax liens and some foreclosures that happen in Athens, but with the university here and its 20,000 students, properties do not get into that spot of being vacant for long and no market for use," Wasserman says.

But in places like Nelsonville, the rehabilitation and restructuring of an older housing stock, and making it appeal to the younger demographic, is key to moving forward. While the little town has the same population as it did in 1900 (about 5,300 people), the local economy has changed drastically. The coal industry is no longer a large employer, and the many businesses associated with that industry have left as well. Oftentimes houses have been abandoned because the original owners have died or have retired elsewhere, and their family is no longer interested in the area.

"Nelsonville is a very poor community that has been hit very hard in the past decades because coal is no longer as important as it used to be," said Chuck Barga, the Nelsonville city manager. "It is very limited for development, because it is landlocked, and no Walmarts or Targets are coming here. For the town to recover economically, it is going to have to become a bedroom community for cities like Logan and Athens.

"But in order to become attractive as a modern-era bedroom community, we have to clean up the housing we have," Barga continued. "We have wonderful old houses, but a dilapidated house is right next to it. It's hard to get people to move here when it is like that, because the dilapidated housing pulls down the value of those around it. People don't want to spend more money on a house than it is going to be worth."

The Athens County Land Bank is able to move the process of this cleanup along faster. When property taxes are delinquent, prospective buyers know the process of obtaining ownership will draw far into the future as the property's financials get cleaned up. And Barga knows that the small town's ability to circumvent those barriers is limited, but the reach of the land bank moves things along.

"Why the land bank appeals to us is it eliminates the delinquent property tax part of the process, and we know that is one of the main problems that hold things up," Barga said.

So what can the future hold for places like Nelsonville? Hocking Hills State Park and the Wayne National Forest are nearby, and they are becoming popular with all-terrain vehicle users, hikers, and bike riders. Ohio University is less than a half-hour drive away for those who work or teach there but want to live in a small town, without the noise of a college town. For smaller towns like Nelsonville, this kind of environment can help the community evolve into the future, rather than dwelling in the past.

"I think we are seeing a real purpose and filling a need in this county," said Chris Chmiel, land bank member and Athens County commissioner. "Having a big university and some wonderful open spaces for recreation and regional tourism are wonderful, but some of these smaller towns need help in dealing with the aging housing."

"It's not that we have to go in and tear down whole blocks of buildings," Chmiel said. "Sometimes it's one here, and another over there, and to help then maybe line up buyers for properties. Community groups are now finding out we are a big asset that they can use in many ways. And in the end, we are finding the people that have lived in these communities for a long time are our best asset. They know what the needs of their community are, and we look to them for the direction to where their biggest needs are."

Clark County Land Bank

In the city of Springfield, Clark County, an abandoned industrial site a few acres large sat just a few miles south of downtown and a few miles north of Interstate 70. The empty lot was in Oakwood Place, a neighborhood in transition, with homes that used to house the workers for the now torn-down industrial facilities, and some large historic homes that were being rehabbed. Plus, it was near a popular bike trail that linked the downtown area to places south.

So what does a land bank do with a few acres of abandoned property like this? Grow sunflowers.

"This is a great example of what can happen when all the players are in a room together," said Ethan Harris, executive director of the Clark County Land Bank. "The land bank has taken it upon itself to work with other organizations and see what we can do to return what is now blighted into productive status."

But why a sunflower field?

The land bank's idea for the sunflower field in Springfield is a classic example of "thinking outside the box." In a meeting between the land bank and other city and county departments a few years ago, this abandoned property came up. Nothing official was decided, but some ideas were thrown around about future use.

"We were talking about recycling in the community, and we started talking about how abandoned land has to be recycled too," said Clark County Solid Waste District Director Chuck Bauer. "So I remembered that

Yellow Springs nearby has a sunflower field as a way to help the environment and preserve property, and I threw out that maybe this property might be good for that."

Leann Castillo, the director of the National Trail Parks and Recreation District, an extensive parks and recreation system in the county, chimed in as well. The district oversaw the bike trails that ran next to the property. She thought something like the sunflower field, which would lessen the maintenance requirements of the property by eliminating the need to mow grass, might work well.

"We also thought people in the neighborhood are protective of where they live, so we thought something different that they could take pride in might be different than just having another vacant lot nearby," Castillo said.

Bauer checked with Yellow Springs to see if they would mind a little "sunflower field competition." They supported the idea, and offered some advice on how to do it right. In the summer of 2018, sunflowers started blooming in the 500 block of West Euclid Avenue in Springfield. They were so tall that people who visited the sunflower field had to look up to see the flowers.

"It was surprising to us how this became an attraction," Castillo said. "People would drive into this neighborhood that they would never come to ordinarily to have their picture taken with the sunflowers. The neighbors helped maintain it and keep it looking wonderful. Kids in the neighborhood were excited because they had never seen anything like it."

The Clark County Land Bank was incorporated in May 2014, and has completed more than 100 demolitions since. They rely on neighbors for input on what the properties should be used for after demolition. The land bank had acquired the sunflower property (now referred to as the Euclid Sunflower Field) as part of its revitalization of vacant and blighted properties. The factory on the site had been demolished several years prior, and the land bank had the remaining concrete foundation slabs removed. When the sunflower field was decided upon as its current short-term use, other agencies worked together to buy and plant the seeds, prepare the soil, and cultivate the growing plants.

The Euclid Sunflower Field has more than 10,000 flowers that bloom each summer, and it draws students and community groups to study bee pollination, as well as how people have used the sunflower throughout history to help clean up the environment. Sunflower fields are touted as sustainable, cost-effective tools for removing contaminants, including chemicals and metals, from soil, water, and air.

Will the sunflower field be permanent? That is yet to be determined, but the land bank and other agencies involved are finding this to be a great transitional use for vacant industrial sites while long-term uses might need some time to gain traction.

"Before the sunflower field was planted, the bike riders on the trail would ride through and never stop at this spot," Castillo said. "Now they do and can see how this older neighborhood really is, how the houses were built around these old factories that aren't here anymore, and we get a real connection between people from different parts of Springfield."

And what is amazing, Castillo says, is that the cell-phone picture-taking phenomenon is driving some of this. "Everyone wants to come here and get their picture taken with sunflowers in the background," she said.

Bauer agreed. "We originally thought of the sunflowers as a good, short-term way of preserving the property and reducing the expenses of maintenance," he said. "Now we are finding it is a place people want to come to, and they can learn about maintaining a clean environment and recycling old properties into new uses and neighborhood revitalization.

"It is amazing," he added, "what can happen with simple ideas turning into something we didn't even think of, and is broader in scope and importance than we ever thought it would be."

Erie County Land Bank

In 2015, Erie County—like many places in Ohio—was experiencing the recent addiction crisis in very real, tangible ways. There were twenty-six overdoses in 2015 in this county of about 75,000 people. The next year, 2016, would be even higher, with thirty-nine overdoses. It was during this time that the Erie County Land Bank took the lead in dealing with the addiction problem through aftercare practices. A condominium complex near Lake Erie in Vermillion Township was in foreclosure due to many units owing about $360,000 in property taxes. A grassroots sober-living organization thought it might be a great place for women with children to live in their early months of sobriety.

But there was a problem. Buying unit by unit to take control of the complex for sober aftercare would take a very long time, and even then, they might only a get a few units and not the entire complex. They needed a public agency to move in and freeze the foreclosure process, mainly to acquire enough of the units to keep them from selling individually at auction.

Through private fundraising, in 2015 Genesis by the Lake (the new name of the facility) foundation members secured the $300,000 necessary to purchase the thirteen acres and eight condominium units that the Erie County Land Bank had acquired. In addition to the $300,000 investment, Genesis also received $280,000 in state funds to help offset costs for refurbishing the complex. The condominiums are in Vermilion Township on U.S. 6 near Beulah Beach, and are now occupied by self-paying women with addiction histories.

Erie County Commissioner Pat Shenigo said at the time, "This is going to be such a great opportunity to help save lives and families here in Erie County. The missing link has always been this: once a person receives treatment, where do they go to live when they return home? Genesis allows women to return to society, have a safe place to live, find and keep a job, and become another successful citizen of Erie County."

Genesis vice president Susan Prentice said that, "If it wasn't for the action of the Erie County Land Bank, this wouldn't have been possible. We wouldn't have even tried to get it without them, because it would have been nearly impossible for us to do it without their help."

Scott Schell, the land bank director, says the addiction aftercare housing facility demonstrates how the whole land bank program movement in Ohio has become about so much more than just demolitions. "We are finding we can be a tool used directly in projects like this, where we are taking a blighted property and finding a good re-use for it without big public costs either," Schell said. "These blighted properties drag down property values of the adjacent neighbor's properties and often become targets of vandalism and break-ins. Eliminating these properties and putting the properties back to productive re-use, helps stabilize, if not increase, neighborhood property values.

"In this case, we are also helping to stabilize a countywide problem that moves into so many areas of our community."

Erie County has some unique property and growth issues. Due to the presence of the nationally renowned Cedar Point amusement park, approximately four million people visit Erie County between May and September. This is also due to the nearby Lake Erie islands and the many commercial and recreational attractions associated with the lake.

But this seasonal population imbalance creates a housing stock problem that the county has grappled with for decades. In the old days, summer cottages, trailers, and cheap hotels dominated the streets in Sandusky. Older buildings also house retail, and have dominated some main drags coming off the Ohio Turnpike. A majority of the housing in Erie County is more than seventy-five years old. Hence, you have places like the MacArthur

Park neighborhood on Sandusky's south side. There are several dozen small houses there that were built in the 1940s, both as a public housing project and for workers at the nearby factory that started out as a munitions factory during the war, and then transformed into a now-defunct car parts production facility.

Sandusky is caught in a tight spot when deciding what to do with these small, out-of-date homes. Tearing them all down would be extremely costly, and it would also leave a big hole in the city that would be difficult to market for economic reuse. But leaving them as-is would perpetuate the problem.

Matt Lasko, the city's chief development officer, explains that the land bank is taking over some properties and demolishing the worst of them "to bring interim green space to the community, but also begin the process of re-envisioning this neighborhood."

Schell said that people need to understand the purpose of land banks in projects like this one. "We do not make policy or implement our own version of urban planning," he says. "But there are times when we are the best option for a city or county to use to get the puzzle pieces to connect. We are finding out there are more and more ways to use land banks, more so than a lot of us originally thought."

Hamilton County Landbank

In the ten years since Ohio authorized counties to create land banks, most counties have leapt on the opportunity, though each set their programs up in different ways. Early on, most land banks were under the umbrella of the general county government. However, as time went on, more land banks were established independent of their county government, including some in unique arrangements based on local preference.

In Hamilton County, with the big city of Cincinnati at its core, the Landbank (they like the singular word down there) was incorporated by the Hamilton County treasurer in October 2011. But by February 2012, the Port of Greater Cincinnati Development Authority ("the Port") was contracted to serve as the management company for this new agency.

The Port is a community and economic development agency that fixes broken real estate. It has three core platforms: industrial revitalization, public finance, and neighborhood revitalization.

Under the Port/Landbank operating agreement, the Landbank pays a management fee, and the Port provides the tools, staffing, expertise, and other resources to efficiently carry out the Landbank's purpose and goals.

What that means in simple terms is that the Landbank has the ability to reach critical mass on many lager projects. Hamilton County's land bank went from the ordinary "tear down homes and create side lots" land bank, to one that focused on neighborhood revitalization connected with existing community groups and economic resources.

This effectively joins together two goals in a way that makes the results more than the sum of their parts. The Port has long been in the property revitalization business with its history of work on economic development projects in Hamilton County. The Landbank, most critically, adds more property acquisition, long-term holding, title clearing and other resources to the Port's arsenal of development tools. Coupled with the Port's ability to raise funds through bonds, its industrial remediation expertise, and strong partnerships with jurisdictions and both non- and for-profit partners, this arrangement opens up more opportunities for what they can do with vacant properties in underutilized neighborhoods.

"We have found that being a part of the Port gives us more flexibility in our work, and leverages a wider range of real estate expertise that has allowed us to think of the big picture in many ways," says Jessica Powell, vice president of the Hamilton County Landbank. "Our work is inherently partnership based. Thus, it doesn't mean we can take over neighborhoods and streets in developing them, but we often are able to work with the community stakeholders more creatively given our involvement in a wide spectrum of real estate development in the county."

The Landbank's Rehab Across Cincinnati and Hamilton County (REACH) program is one example of how this has played out in Hamilton County. Through REACH, the Landbank rehabs vacant and blighted housing stock in one focus neighborhood to kickstart a dormant housing market. Years of neglect and disinvestment has made this approach to revitalization critical due to the risk of investment being too high for the private market. Under REACH, investment is done strategically at scale—which lowers cost and creates critical mass. The end result is the creation of new market comps that position the neighborhood for future investment.

The Landbank's first REACH neighborhood was Evanston. The old neighborhood has a population that is mostly African-American and is situated along Interstate 71, five miles north of the Cincinnati downtown, and includes Xavier University on its northern edge.

A Landbank-funded study in 2014 looked at both strengths and weaknesses in this neighborhood. The majority of units in the neighborhood were single family, many of them large historic homes between 2,000 and

3,500 square feet in size. But there was also a high poverty level among residents, housing stock was hard hit by the foreclosure crisis, and there was a very high vacancy rate (23 percent) coupled with a high cost of renovation. Most telling of all, there had not been one market-rate sale of a home in nine years.

The study showed that "[m]any current buyers and rental operators [did] not have the means to properly renovate units which also contribute[d] to the lack of maintenance and 'curb appeal' that could attract new home buyers with the means to complete full renovations." Long-time homeowners in the neighborhood were unable to refinance their homes, secure money for home repairs, or even pass equity on to future generations.

Using data from the Evanston study, the Landbank worked with neighborhood groups and longtime residents to identify streets that had large concentrations of vacant and blighted structures that were candidates for rehab. Once it defined its focus geography, the Landbank acquired more than forty vacant blighted single-family homes and over the course of five years, rehabbed and sold twenty-five of those, in addition to constructing five infill homes on former vacant lots.

"In the past, the county's main option for dealing with foreclosed properties was to auction them off to the highest bidder. More often than not, this meant the transfer of the property to out-of-town investors and property owners with a track record of poor property stewardship," Powell says. "With the Landbank in place, we are able to acquire blighted, vacant properties; avoid property speculation; and work with neighborhood stakeholders to determine the best path for a property. And in some neighborhoods, this means that we need to hold properties for a while until the market develops such that there is private interest or we secure funds to subsidize rehab."

The Landbank's success with REACH in the Evanston neighborhood has since been applied in other neighborhoods in Cincinnati, including Walnut Hills, Avondale, and Price Hill. In the latter two, rehab funds have been secured through grants from Children's Hospital and the City of Cincinnati.

With stabilizing housing markets in the Landbank's REACH neighborhoods has come the opportunity to leverage other Landbank and Port resources. The Port's public finance tools have been deployed to help finance a brewery in Walnut Hills and the rehab of a masonic temple in Price Hill. In all three neighborhoods, the Landbank has deployed its historic stabilization tools and the Port's Homesteading and Urban

Revitalization Program (HURC) has done over a dozen affordable single-family rehabs.

Since its inception, the biggest challenge—and opportunity—for the Landbank is to continue to work with neighborhood stakeholders to improve their communities in a way that makes them feel included and uplifted by the changes around them. In partnership with others, the Landbank is glad to be at the helm of positive community change.

Lawrence County Land Bank

It was an odd distinction in some ways.

In Lawrence County, a county in the most southern part of Ohio, on the Ohio River and home to the city of South Point (so named for an obvious reason), 40 percent of the housing units are trailers. So, when it came time to use money from the Neighborhood Initiative Program (NIP) to conduct demolitions, there was a bit of a catch.

"The NIP didn't think trailers really could be torn down, not really houses or homes, and they didn't qualify for the program," said Tom Schneider, the administrator of operations for the Lawrence County Land Bank. "We had to explain to them that trailers are not always on wheels, and removing them can be as tough as doing a home. We believe we were the first to get trailers qualified for demolition from the NIP funding."

Lawrence County is not unique in how its demographics and economy have changed in recent decades. It used to be a center for iron, timber, coal, and salt mining-based industries; its location on the Ohio River was perfect for these industries. Many of those resources were depleted over time in the twentieth century, and industries left because of technological and economic changes as well as the aging population. Today, in many ways Lawrence County and all its little towns on the river have become bedroom communities for larger Kentucky communities across the river, like Huntington.

Some of the abandoned homes that were left behind, trailers included, have since become drug-use and sale hubs for the opioid drug epidemic that has festered in this part of the U.S.

"The drug problem was something that was tough to get our hands on because the dealers and users would come across the river, set up shop in an abandoned house, let the drug users know they were open for business, and then go back across the river when they were done," said Lawrence County Treasurer Stephen Burcham, chairman of the land bank board.

"We had several teardown projects where we had to load up trailers full of needles and prescription drug containers just to start the process of getting rid of the eyesore," he said. "It was one of the ways that the land bank is being very useful in this community.

"The law enforcement officials and health care professionals see we are making a huge difference in the communities here," he said.

The Lawrence County Land Bank began in 2016 and has had some unique geographic challenges to deal with. The county is large in area—450 square miles, but has a relatively small population of about 60,000, with the county seat of Ironton at 12,000 people. Some areas are very historic, going back to the early 1800s. The hilly terrain and Ohio River make isolation of some communities a natural occurrence, and the poverty rate—like most Ohio counties along the Ohio River—is above the national average.

At times, the projects the land bank takes on are very specific. For example, take the Pulley Nursing Home in Burlington that had been abandoned for more than a decade and burdened those who live around it. "I've been here for fifty years, and I've seen that place when it was a functioning building, and more lately, an abandoned nuisance," said Simon Gore, who lives next door. "It was disheartening to see what you're living next to, but it was great to see it torn down." He then joked that he doesn't see as many raccoons on his property anymore.

Other projects are just as simple. One old abandoned home near a little league baseball field was torn down in the town of Chesapeake and the land was given to the little league to use as an entrance park to their field. Many such teardowns free up space that can be remarketed for new buildings, or just for open space where there was once a neighborhood eyesore.

"What we are able to do is move the process along faster and I think the public and local governments see the advantage in that," Burcham said. "I know as the treasurers we are seeing delinquencies come off the rolls, and also seeing a savings in all the cost the local communities are paying out, in law enforcement and health care and declining property values near these vacant homes."

As far as the trailers go, there are a few restrictions the government put on using public funds to tear them down. The mobile homes must be "affixed," meaning attached to an existing home or one that is not mobile and sinking into the ground. If it is mobile, then it can still be removed under the NIP program, but anything that can be recycled must be. The amount of recycling cash can be small—$350 per trailer moved out—but that can add up.

"What we are finding is that neighborhoods see us as a real asset now as they see what we do," Schneider said. "Many communities are very small and get the feeling they are on their own. But we are able to come around and help them out with some primary needs they had trouble dealing with.

"Sometimes things are real simple. An abandoned house blocks a baseball field. We tear it down and give it to them. They use it to make the neighborhood look better. And in the end, it is much better now than it was before."

Lucas County Land Bank

For many years, city and county government officials in Toledo, Ohio wondered what to do with the empty Haughton Elevator Company factory next to the Toledo Zoo. The factory had been shut down since 1989, and had devolved into twenty-two fenced-in acres of broken concrete and twisted metal. And if that wasn't enough of a problem, the owners of the property owed $100,000 in back taxes.

"It was vacant and everyone noticed it, because it was both a sign of the manufacturing base we used to have more of, and it was right next to next to one of our places that people were very proud of," said David Mann, president of the Lucas County Land Bank. "If you were coming to the zoo, you'd see this vacant lot first. And no one knew what to do with it."

In 2014, the county land bank was able to untangle the delinquent tax issues and other title issues to the land itself. They found an energy company that quietly had their eyes on the property, and the land bank was able to be the matchmaker between the new owner and the county tax assessor's office. In the end, the energy company got the property they needed, cleaned up the acreage, put in about 30,000 solar panels, and now provides 30 percent of the zoo's electricity annually.

"The role we played in this is that we were the catalyst to make this happen," Mann said. "Maybe the energy company could have figured it out, but economically, they needed a fresh start and cut the timeline down in order to do this work. We could do that, and as a result, we were able to clean up some decayed property and provide renewable energy for the area."

Initially, the Ohio legislature granted Cuyahoga County the authority to create a county land bank, and its land bank was launched in July 2009. Following passage of a law in early 2010, land banking authority was extended to all Ohio counties with populations greater than 60,000. In August 2010, Lucas County became the second county in Ohio to create a land reutilization corporation (LRC). In July 2016, the Lucas County Land Bank launched an ambitious campaign to renovate or demolish 1,500 properties in as many days. When the 1,500th day arrived in the summer of 2019, the land bank had easily surpassed that goal and as of April 2020 had renovated or demolished more than 2,200 properties.

"A lot of people think that the land bank is about that vacant house that has to be either demolished or rehabbed, in reality it is not about that house, it's about all of the other homes on the block that have seen their values go down when a vacant, blighted home comes in," said Toledo Mayor Wade Kapszukiewicz.

But the Lucas County Land Bank is also finding that neighborhoods can use some help on bigger projects. One is St. Anthony's Catholic Church, built in 1894, just a few miles southwest of downtown Toledo in the Junction neighborhood. The church, architecturally, is a pure gothic structure of brick, 92 feet wide and 158 feet long. The roof is 120 feet high, and the tower is an incredible 250 feet high. Ten pillars support the steep roof. The parish church seats about 1,600 people for services, and the property also includes other structures that once housed clergy and provided meeting places.

It hasn't had any liturgical services there since 2005. The church for years had been slated for demolition by the diocese, but community groups and elected officials advocated for the building to be preserved and repurposed as a focal point for the neighborhood. In 2018, the Lucas County Land Bank and the Roman Catholic Diocese of Toledo agreed to have the land bank take ownership of the property after years of the diocese considering tearing it down. The church once catered to a large Polish community in Toledo, but the ethnic congregation that once lived in the neighborhood is no longer. Now the church is in a very poor neighborhood with numerous vacant lots nearby. "We are not sure what [the church] will become, but we are open to working with the community around it to help meet their needs," Mann said.

The Pythian Castle, on Jefferson Avenue and Ontario Street downtown, built in 1890 by the fraternal organization Knights of Pythias, has also been saved from demolition by the land bank. The building is about five stories tall, and features a textured sandstone exterior, a conical roof, arched windows and a tower. Inside, there is an auditorium, ballroom, and over 30,000 square feet of space. The most recent occupant was an arts center in the 1970s.

The land bank acquired the historic structure in 2013 through a deed-in-lieu of foreclosure and sold it in 2016 to a developer for $300. Renovation has been on and off since then, but the developer expects lowers floors will be commercial, while the upper floors would function well as either residential or commercial when finished. The land bank has set some renovation timeline goals that must be met by the developer, or the building will revert back to the land bank.

"The Pythian Castle is a historic treasure, and once restoration is finished, it can be a great addition to a part of downtown Toledo that is growing," Mann said.

Mahoning County Land Bank

When Hakem Al-Mhairat saw the old house, he wasn't thinking of a suburban-status home that a young man with a lovely wife and three children (and a fourth on the way) would be thinking of. He was thinking more about how to save money on rent.

Al-Mhairat was paying about $750 a month rent for the space his family needed, and they felt squeezed by other visiting family members needing a place to stay. He and his wife, both from Syria, were in healthcare graduate programs at Youngstown State University, and were often alternating the many time constraints of childcare, working, and studies—with visiting relatives thrown in on top of that.

So Al-Mhairat decided to buy a fixer-upper through the Mahoning County Land Bank. He paid about $7,500 for the three-bedroom house and had agreed to contribute about $30,000 to get it up to standards. He was doing much of that work himself, and the land bank would not transfer the title to him until it passed inspection within a designated time frame.

At times it has been frustrating for him and his wife, but they know it will pay off in the long term for them. "I never thought I'd be laying tile in a kitchen," he said in his kitchen, laughing. "But even though this place needs work, it is in a nice neighborhood near the university, and has a big enough backyard for the kids to play. And the neighbors we have met have been very nice to us."

Founded in 2011, the Mahoning County Land Bank is broadening its reach as an economic development tool not only to help blighted neighborhoods, but to boost the vitality of commercial corridors in the Mahoning Valley. That means matching up buyers and homes, and in some cases, the land bank's reach has even expanded to influence the creation and retention of jobs and businesses that otherwise would have relocated because of the housing problems.

"We're getting encouragement from parties to be a player in economic development going forward— not as a developer— but in a supporting role," said Debora Flora, executive director of the Mahoning County Land Bank. "That includes having people move back into neighborhoods that need the investment of good people who want to invest in the city with home ownership that they can do with sweat equity if they need to."

The land bank has been demolishing houses since 2015 as part of a program to bring relief to neighbors and municipal leaders, who have had to take care of abandoned houses and vacant lots due to lack of action by the owners. The land bank has completed 1,110 demolitions as of 2020. The land bank has also aided in the renovation of about seventy-five houses in partnership with the Youngstown Neighborhood Development Corporation. As part of this, the land bank will acquire and assemble land for business startups and expansions, and convert vacant places in strategic locations to green spaces.

One good example of a park development occurred in 2017 at Erie Street and East Judson Avenue, in the Pleasant Grove neighborhood south of downtown Youngstown. An obsolete six-unit residence was torn down and converted into an attractive park at that intersection.

"The demolition of a vacant house is just the first step to what we do as land banks," said Flora. "But our mission as a whole is to establish how we can make these spaces productive again. Whether that is working with community groups to install bus stops or create flexible parks where children and neighbors can gather for games, picnics or reading books from the little free libraries located there—we work with individuals in the communities to find out what those neighborhoods need."

These "neighborhood action plans" may be having the effect of reducing vacancies and the need for teardowns. A recent study by Youngstown State University found home vacancies across the city were down "dramatically" and property values are "slightly up" since the neighborhood plans were implemented in 2014.

Ian Beniston, executive director of the Youngstown Neighborhood Development Corporation, said that the rate of vacancies across the city has fallen. "Vacancies have gone down dramatically. In 2008, there were about 4,600 vacant homes. In 2014, there were still 3,900 vacant homes, despite thousands of demolitions. We were barely keeping up," said Beniston. "Over the last five years since we enacted the action plans, we saw the number go from 3,900 to 2,200. So a 43 percent reduction. That's huge."

Flora is seeing the changes as well, and the role of the land bank is evolving with those changes. "The creation of Mahoning County Land Bank was neither coincidental nor convenient," the former journalist wrote in an op-ed in 2019. "Motivated residents pressed state senators and representatives to approve enabling legislation in 2010, so that the pilot land bank in Cuyahoga County could be replicated. New collaborations between public, private, and nonprofit entities became necessary. Trust had to be established between partners, some past practices were set aside, and channels of communication were opened with funders.

"Mahoning County is in long-term recovery from property vacancy and abandonment. The pool of distressed housing is shrinking, but the neighbors of remaining empty, blighted houses still seek relief. Resources also will be needed to remove or repurpose vacant commercial properties to enhance neighborhood revitalization and business development."

Perry County Land Bank

When coal ruled supreme in the Appalachian regions of this country, beginning in the 1800s and extending into the 1960s, many small mining towns and townships sprung up in southeastern Ohio, particularly in Athens, Hocking, and Perry Counties. Some of these communities came to be known as the "Little Cities of Black Diamonds," an acknowledgement of the role the Black Diamond Company played in the development of towns around their coal mines. A local newspaper reporter used this phrase to describe Nelsonville of Athens County in the late nineteenth century. An Ohio University professor wrote a dissertation on this region in the 1970s and used this phrase again—and it stuck.

Perry County, because of its population size, was not eligible to form a county land bank until the fall of 2015. They incorporated the land bank in 2017 to take advantage of the demolition funding from the Hardest Hit Fund that was made available through the U.S. Department of the Treasury. Initially, the program was run by David Hanson, the county's director of economic development. However, Drew Cannon, the county auditor, generated much of the excitement around the program. He has been actively involved in identifying properties and helping to advance the land bank's operations. As of 2020, the land bank had completed over fifty demolitions.

Perry County's land bank has also developed a unique relationship with their health department, which receives significant dollars each year from the Tunnel Hill Reclamation Landfill in New Lexington. The landfill is advertised as the largest by rail landfill company in the United States, with the capacity for 8,000 tons of construction and demolition landfill waste per day. This waste comes from as far away as Massachusetts. The fees generated total more than $2 million a year, and because of the existence of the Perry County Land Bank and the capacity they have developed, the health department has diverted $200,000 to the land bank for the demolition of blighted properties.

Chad Cook has worked with the Perry County health department for nineteen years as a Sanitarian. He has been dealing with blighted, nuisance properties for much of his career, and for him the land bank has provided a badly needed relief valve for these nuisance properties.

"We had funding to do these demolitions earlier, but we had no way to deal with the delinquent taxes. We didn't want to own property. We didn't want to be in the real estate business. The land bank was our answer."

What has been particularly encouraging to Drew Cannon is how much activity has been spurred by the land bank's clean-up efforts and how the work of the land bank has infused energy—and hope—in a town like New Lexington.

"Hundreds of thousands of dollars have been spent by private land owners because of the work that has been done by the land bank in removing blighted properties. I know of numerous examples where private land owners removed blighted properties that they owned because of the example set by the land bank."

The auditor pointed to two examples on Main Street in New Lexington of business expansions that he thinks are directly attributable to the land bank's efforts in blight removal.

"Shortly after we began taking abandoned homes down on Main Street one owner of a complex that included a sandwich shop, laundromat, and a car wash acquired dilapidated adjoining properties and tore them down to protect his investment. Not far away the owner of a gas station and convenience store did the same thing."

Cannon pointed out that the blight removal efforts of the land bank have resulted in numerous owners of empty and substandard properties reaching out to demolition contractors at the site of demolitions and getting quotes to take down their own structures.

"This has had a ripple effect, for sure. I also know of homes that had been on the market, but pulled for lack of activity. Many of these homes have gone back on the market because we have created a better environment."

Richland County Land Bank

About two-and-a-half miles north of downtown Mansfield is the now-closed Ohio State Reformatory, where the film *The Shawshank Redemption*, released in 1994, was shot. The "Shawshank Tree," a huge white oak located near Malabar Farm State Park in Lucas, Ohio, was about seven miles southwest of downtown Mansfield in Richland County. The tree was at least 100 feet tall and approximately 180 to 200 years old. It was split by lightning on July 29, 2011 and was eventually knocked down by strong winds on or around July 22, 2016. The tree is famous as being the place in the film where the character Ellis Boyd "Red" Redding (Morgan Freeman) read the letter from Andy Dufresne (Tim Robbins) after he was paroled.

"Remember Red, hope is a good thing, maybe the best of things, and no good thing ever dies," Dufresne wrote.

2019 marked the twenty-fifth anniversary of the film, and Mansfield celebrated it with a reunion of actors from the film and a showing at Mansfield's downtown Renaissance Theatre, previously known as the Ohio Theatre—a restored movie theater originally opened on January 18, 1928. What most people attending the film's anniversary activities in Mansfield didn't realize is that the restored movie theater is part of a resurrected downtown area called "Imagination District," and that the Richland County Land Bank played a big role in recent development of this part of downtown.

The Renaissance purchased the 15,000-square-foot building from the land bank for $89 in December 2016. The old and abandoned building (which had housed a variety of businesses through the years) was in such bad shape that HAZMAT suits were required to walk through the space. The movie theater company, however, saw this new building as a key to its expansion of arts in the central city.

The new black box theatre called Theatre 166, is also in a formerly decrepit old building, only two doors down from the old Renaissance Theatre. It opened in 2018 and serves as a gathering place for actors, artists, musicians, and art advocates. The intimate space—only 125 seats—allows for the cultivation of original works, new interpretations of overlooked masterpieces, and re-examination of seldom-seen classics. It is almost as if Mansfield, Ohio has an arts movie theater of the sort usually only found in small college towns or huge artistic cities.

While the theater company had been looking to expand in previous years, it was not until the land bank approached them that they advanced their plans into the next stage.

"At first people were telling us that we needed to get more property and tear down buildings for parking spaces and we never saw things that way," said Michael Miller, president & CEO of the Renaissance Performing

Arts Association. "What the people from the land bank showed us was how we could revitalize this pretty much useless building and expand our footprint in downtown Mansfield.

"It became a no-brainer for us and we are so pleased with what has developed," he continued. "A derelict property has been transformed into an arts center that can house artists working on summer stock theater, and a place to have classes for people interested in movie making. The land bank took the lead on this because they saw the bigger picture, and they helped us to see it too."

The Richland County Land Bank has also been instrumental in property acquisitions for the Little Buckeye Children's Museum, located near the Renaissance Theatre expansion. "What we are seeing is that our role as a facilitator can be a real impetus for moving forward on projects that maybe weren't completely desirable without us involved," said land bank manager Amy Hamrick.

Since it was created in 2013, the Richland County Land Bank has sold about fifty properties through its Residential Rehabilitation Program. These properties are sold typically for $1,000 and are restored by the new owner. The land bank had handled more than 500 demolitions as well. The average cost of a demolition in Richland County is $12,444.10.

The challenge for Mansfield and Richland County, like many other places in Ohio, is the demographic and economic changes they are experiencing. There has been a slight decline in population over time (about 16 percent in Mansfield since 1970), and some of the manufacturing businesses have either closed or relocated. However, the county houses three large food companies and is becoming a large employer for the regional health care industry.

"What we are finding," Hamrick said, "is that we do have some population decline and need less housing, and are making the choices to rehab or teardown some of the older homes to get the market more in line with what we need.

"But we are also seeing that our downtown area has great potential for growth right now and we can help organizations and businesses make those investments," she said. "And what we are seeing through the Imagination District is that people want to look forward and not just redo the past. That's very exciting for Mansfield and Richland County."

Scioto County Land Bank

Portsmouth has always been a hub for river traffic. It is where the Scioto and Ohio rivers meet, and that spot was among the first in the modern

United States to join traffic from the portages of the Great Lakes to the deltas of the Mississippi Rivers. Over time, it became the center or iron and steel forges, brick making, and, of all things, shoe manufacturing. But these days, the population has dropped to about 20,000 (about half what it was in the 1940s) and the city is in flux. In its heyday Portsmouth was the home of the one of largest outdoor pools in America. Known as "Dreamland," it was part of a larger recreational complex known throughout the region. *Dreamland* was also the title of a 2015 book by Sam Quinones that talked about the decline of the area and the growth of the opioid and black tar heroin addiction problem. (The recreation complex closed in the 1990s—and was demolished.)

The Scioto County Land Bank operates with both history and future on its mind. In downtown Portsmouth, for example, it helped acquire an old building that will be turned into a pocket park. This project is unique in that the façade of the building will be kept as an entrance, with the pocket park behind it. At the same time, teardowns are in order. Older neighborhoods east and south of downtown and the Ohio River have more abandoned properties. Some are on streets that wind through hillsides and are tough to get to, but they still affect the nearby neighbors who have been dealing with this abandonment for a long time.

"It's not an easy proposition as sometimes it takes a lot of entities to gain ownership of these blighted properties," said Scioto County Commissioner and land bank chair Bryan Davis. "The cooperation between the county, city, villages, and townships has been amazing. For the most part, everyone is supporting the work being done and understands why it is important to clean up our area."

In regards to the conditions of the homes, Davis said that these dwellings are unlivable and unsafe: "They're all really bad. That's something I hope everybody understands: these are houses that have actually gone through sheriff's sales. These are the worst of the worst; nobody wants these houses. We're getting rid of the blight, we're cleaning up the neighborhood, and we're getting these properties back on the tax rolls, and we have people that are buying these lots and plan on building on them. That's how you rejuvenate a community."

The Scioto County Land Bank has been operating since 2016 and has recently hit its 100th demolition.

This historical county is working with neighborhood groups to move the process forward. If a house is demolished, the property can be sold to an adjacent property owner for $200. Sometimes more than one property owner has interest, and the lot can be split up. Other times, neighbors don't want the lot and there are other options.

"Some examples of use could be for economic development, a community garden, basketball courts or another type of community relation project," Davis said. One good example of how these ideas come to fruition is the teardown of an old house downtown near the Scioto River. The house was abandoned near an American Legion post. Out of some informal meetings came the idea to tear the old house down and give it to the post.

"What they were able to do is clear it all out, reseed the lot, and save some of the larger trees," said Emmett Gregory of Post 23. "We think it's great. Anytime you can expand it's wonderful." He says they'll start out with some with some picnic tables, but perhaps transform it into a public park for people in the community.

The land bank has also seen vacant lots transformed into community gardens; lots were given over to a local church food pantry to grow food for the needy, and two additional lots near a downtown community center have been turned into a community garden intended to teach children the joys of gardening and raising their own food.

One of the other problems the land bank is addressing in Portsmouth is the opioid epidemic. Scioto and other counties in Ohio became early center points for pill mill drug providers and addicts.

In 2018, local registered nurse Lisa Roberts and coordinator of the Scioto County Drug Action Team Alliance testified before Congress on the uniqueness and seriousness of the problem.

"In 2010, Scioto County has the highest prescription opioid distribution rate in Ohio and the highest fatal overdose rate in the state at more than double the state average. We also had the highest rate of infants born with neonatal abstinence syndrome and numerous other community problems related to opioid addiction. And like so many parents, my own child developed an opioid use disorder at a young age and has struggled mightily with this disease throughout adulthood. It has been a long and difficult struggle for my family."

The problem is still around, but improving, and Davis wants the land bank to be a part of the solution.

"With our opioid epidemic, we're seeing a lot of people living in condemned houses," Davis said. "There's a lot of drug activity in those homes, a lot of illegal activities in those houses. We're also finding children that are in those conditions and by tearing these houses down, we make them less of a target for people to live in them illegally.

"I think when people come into our community, they're going to see a nice community, they're going to see homes that are kept up, they're not going to see the burned-out homes and the vacant properties," Davis said. "They're going to see a good area where people can live and play and be able to enjoy life, and that's our goal."

Trumbull County Land Bank

Sam Lamancusa remembers exactly when the need for a land bank in Trumbull County made real sense to him. It was early 2010, and the Trumbull County Treasurer had been observing some property auctions at the courthouse, seeing the usual transactions. Houses and apartment buildings in property tax foreclosure were selling for pennies on the dollar of what they were really worth.

"There was nothing new with that," he said. "I had long been frustrated that we were actually losing money on these auctions, because the title transfer wasn't paying the taxes, and it just seemed to me we were just transferring property from one bad landlord to another most of the time." On his way home, he decided to check out one of the homes sold for about $7,500 to see what it looked like. He was amazed at what he saw.

"The guy who had just bought it had a broken window and big problems on the exterior from what I could see, and he was putting up a "for rent" sign and asking about $500 a month," he said. "First off, that was illegal to do so, to try to rent a house that couldn't pass basic codes. So driving home, it bothered me, and I kept thinking that this auction process wasn't doing anything to fix the problems. Maybe we needed some major changes in how we deal with property like this.

"The people that thought we should look at starting a land bank like Cuyahoga County had finally started making sense to me, mainly because of what I saw that afternoon."

So the Trumbull County Land Bank was formed. But Trumbull County has changed the traditional land bank organization a bit over time. The treasurer's office initially ran the entirety of the land bank operations, but has had different programs farmed out so that it would not just become a demolition arm of the property tax foreclosure part of Lamancusa's office. "I could see early on that we had to get neighborhood groups involved more, because they would know what would work and what would not in their neighborhoods," he said.

Much of the work is now done under the Trumbull Neighborhood Partnership (TNP) umbrella, a 501(c)3 nonprofit community development organization focused on neighborhood revitalization in the city of Warren and surrounding communities. It was awarded the contract to manage the land bank in 2013. It was an obvious fit as both organizations had a shared mission of revitalizing neighborhoods and increasing the quality of life for residents, but with the land bank being operated by TNP there was the opportunity to pursue different funding opportunities not always available to land banks, or vice versa.

Initially, TNP's programming was heavily volunteer-driven, with more than 300 residents donating more than 1,600 hours to board up vacant homes, pick up trash, install public art, and establish community gardens and pocket parks. This systematically addressed blight and decay by improving the landscape, all while increasing pride and ownership in the city of Warren's neighborhoods.

The volunteer efforts were highly successful, but as TNP grew, they decided to provide skills-based training and employment for residents as the neighborhood revitalization strategies presented the opportunity. The different aspects of overseeing housing issues—renovation, deconstruction, landscape installation, and vacant property maintenance—made having an able-paid workforce living in these neighborhoods to do this work more important.

"A lot of time urban planning people often think they either need already established local political agencies or volunteers to do the work, but we found that we needed real employees under our umbrella, because the work we needed to do was very multidimensional," said Matt Martin, executive director of Trumbull Neighborhood Partnership. "We need people who can do a lot of different things, and who know the needs of the Trumbull County neighborhoods personally."

"What we have found is that there are often tons of opinions and studies, or anecdotes about whose fault the housing crisis is, but at the end of the day, the burden of what has happened falls squarely on the shoulders of the next-door neighbor, the block, the neighborhood, and the community," says Shawn Carvin, Trumbull County Land Bank director. "That is what we are addressing, and why we are doing it as we are."

So, as Carvin said, "Sometimes you have to tear down two houses to save one, but in other cases it's the renovation of two homes on a street to stabilize market values."

As an example of that home-saving mentality, TNP is expanding into emergency home repairs for low-income homeowners. It is a countywide program of emergency replacement of essential home-related components such as furnaces, roofing and hot-water tanks, and further seeks to improve accessibility for homeowners with disabilities. Homeowners eligible for assistance must have income at or below fifty percent of the area median income. For example, a family of four can earn $30,700 or less per year and be eligible. A single person can earn $21,700 or less. Up to $7,500 can be provided to each homeowner. They hope to help fifty homeowners each year, supplementing the renovation and demolition efforts on vacant homes in the same neighborhoods.

"What we are finding is that the old sense of neighborhoods where people care can drive things so much better than the assumption that people don't," Lamancusa said. "We are making great progress by using the caring neighborhood residents as an asset we use, instead of viewing these neighborhood activists as an impediment we don't want to deal with.

"I remember growing up in the town of Girard in this county and we all knew what everyone was up to in our neighborhood and that was healthy," he continued. "The way the land bank is set up by us, we can take advantage of that basic way people think and care. It makes so much sense to set it up that way."

Martin says progress has been made, but the need for federal housing grant funds remains and the use of funding may need to be tweaked. Right now, the money is mostly for demolition.

"Demolition gets rid of the worst properties, and we are doing that, but it doesn't help with the middle ones, which we also need to address," Martin said. "We're going to get stuck in a position where we have more houses than money to renovate them."

Van Wert County Land Bank

As the program manager for the Thomas Edison Center adult programs in Van Wert County, Ohio, a day service for people with developmental disabilities, Carla Frank has long networked with the area's businesses and political leadership to find ways to make room for their clients in local workplaces.

Frank and the Thomas Edison Center board members have always had a simple and singular goal in mind: community inclusion for their adult clients. That meant getting them vocational training and enhancing work related skills: attendance, responsibility, task completion, problem solving, social interaction, and workplace safety.

And that's where the Van Wert County Land Bank came into play.

"We were doing what we always do, going to local events and meetings, and we just started talking with the land bank people in what was really just basic conversation," Frank said. "They were fairly new, and our early conversations were nothing more than friendly talks over coffee and trying to get to know them and what they do better.

"But we realized pretty quickly some needs we both shared, that were really so simple and basic, but purposeful as well," she continues. "They had properties that needed the exteriors maintained—mostly by mowing lawns and doing some outdoor cleaning. We had mentally disabled adults who we had on crews that did those things. Our people could use the work, and they had work that needed to be done. So we hooked up on that."

Stacy Adam, the executive director of the Van Wert Area Economic Development Corporation since January 2017, oversees the land bank work. She concurred about the needs and "community inclusion."

"What we have found in the relatively short time we have been doing our job in Van Wert County is that we are more than just a home demolitions program or an agency that passes properties back and forth solely based on property tax foreclosures," she said. "In this case, we found that there was a time frame where we needed to hold on to some properties and make them look fine in the neighborhood while we sorted out the options for what we would do with them.

So, not only were we able to do that work completed by contracting with the Thomas Edison School, we were able to contribute to the community by using their clients in a way that helped them and helped us," she said. "Because one thing we, and the other land bank directors I have spoken with, have figured out is that one of the main things that keeps our community support going is to work with the neighborhoods and the community. So they see us as an asset and not just an agency that handles property tax issues."

The Van Wert County Land Bank has only been operative since 2017, when the state made the land bank program available to smaller counties. Van Wert is in northwestern Ohio, near the Indiana border, and has a population just under 30,000. Over the years, it has been a mixture of rural and small towns, with about 10,000 of the county population living in the city of Van Wert. The population numbers have been virtually unchanged since 1950.

But the housing has been aging in the county, due to a lack of growth in both population and industrial businesses. On some of the streets in the county seat, there is an odd mix; on one street near the downtown Van Wert area, there stands a classic early 1900s home with a large wrap-around porch with columns, next to a smaller single-family home in serious need of exterior repair and with junk in the yard, which is in turn next to a run-down brick apartment building that looks like it was built in the 1950s.

"Revitalization is infectious," said JoAnne Simmerman, the land bank manager at a recent county meeting. "The process not only restores property values but also restores hope and pride in one's neighborhood. The process is guided by respect for historic sites and care for the residents of the surrounding homes."

In its three years of existence, the Van Wert County Land Bank has acquired about seventy-five properties throughout the county and revitalized some of those that were vacant and blighted. Many have been torn down. Certain properties are sold to the general public and others offered to owners of land adjacent to the lot being sold by the land bank.

The Van Wert Land Bank has received $1.65 million in federal grant funds since it was formed in 2017. Land bank activity has led to a decline in the county's tax delinquency rate from 2.7 percent in 2016 to 1.3 percent in 2018. The important impact, however, is more than just the small change in the accounting balance ledger in the annual county reports. Van Wert County and its citizens are seeing that the land bank is a valuable asset with various purposes and the ability to connect different agencies and business interests.

"I realize it's easy to let properties go over a period of time, and it's even easier over time to accept them as normal for our community," said Paul Hoverman, director of the Niswonger Performing Arts Center in Van Wert. "However, when a new eye comes into our community and makes us aware of how it could be, we all benefit. Through the land bank operation, Van Wert has been able to raze certain buildings and homes in disarray that many have become accustomed to. What an improvement we have experienced with the elimination and return to green space of these blighted properties."

In April 2019, the Van Wert County Foundation undertook the daunting task of helping to rebuild the downtown of the city of Van Wert by getting into the real estate acquisition business, and not by buying one or two distressed properties—but ultimately buying over fifty buildings in the downtown area.

Seth Baker, the executive secretary of the foundation, also served on the Business Development Corporation (BDC) for Van Wert. They were constantly discussing the distressed condition of the buildings in downtown Van Wert—and what to do with them. They discussed buying an individual building or two, but consulted with developers who had undertaken a similar project thirty miles away in Fort Wayne, Indiana. The consensus was clear: to attract a big developer they would have to acquire dozens of properties and in effect 'bundle' them for the developer.

They have acquired almost forty buildings thus far and spent $3 million. Their goal is to acquire fifty-five buildings in total. They have developer interest and hope to use the Van Wert County Land Bank strategically—to hold distressed properties until they can put together a combination of historic and new market tax credits to make the redevelopment of some of these buildings economically viable. The foundation has already transferred the troubled Homeguard building to the land bank as part of this plan.

Chapter Nine:
Where Do We Go from Here?

Jim Rokakis

As of the writing of this book, fifty-seven Ohio counties had established county land reutilization corporations, or county land banks, as they are commonly known. What began as a single county "hail Mary pass," almost a desperate last-ditch response to deal with the aftermath of the foreclosure crisis, has grown into a statewide network that has reached every corner of Ohio—urban, suburban, and rural. What began as an Ohio and Michigan response to the Great Recession, has now become part of a larger, national movement with land banks of some nature at play in seventeen states.

How did this happen?

There are many reasons for the growth of land banks in Ohio—and nationally. Let's start with this first reason: land banks work. They have proved to be successful at quickly acquiring vacant and abandoned properties, and in many cases repurposing them quickly. Land banks focus in primarily on the worst of properties—properties that are abandoned and tax delinquent; properties that very often will require demolition. These are properties that nobody particularly wants, but their impact on surrounding properties can be devastating. The ability to deal with these properties quickly can be the difference between a neighborhood stabilizing—or falling into further despair.

But that leads to an equally important reason for the success of land banks in Ohio, and that has to do with the hundreds of millions of dollars that have been raised giving these land banks the resources to deal with these blighted properties. The blighted property problem in "Rust Belt" states like Ohio, Indiana, and Michigan—and others—is a multi-billion-dollar problem. When we began organizing land banks on Ohio we estimated that approximately 100,000 structures had been abandoned, had become tax delinquent, and were facing potential demolition. There were thousands of abandoned commercial structures including factories, warehouses, abandoned hospitals, schools, shopping strips, and apartment buildings.

There was no public funding source for blight removal until this movement began. There are lobbyists for new home construction in Washington D.C. and state capitals all over the country. There are lobbyists for the home remodeling industry and the manufactured home industry. But I have yet to meet a single lobbyist for blight removal. The issue of blighted properties has never gathered the singular focus of policy makers in spite of the devastating impact these eyesores—and sometimes death traps—have had on communities and their property tax bases. Land banks and the land bank movement have become, in effect, the lobbyist for blight removal and are dealing with it in a systematic fashion, as opposed on a case by case basis at the local government level—where communities are strapped and able to deal with only the worst of the worst—often after a tragedy.

Of course, bringing back communities with blighted properties is about more than just demolition. Thousands of properties have been renovated in Ohio and across the country through the intervention of land banks. And because of the safeguards land banks have put into place these renovations have been more than a slipshod "slapping on a coat of paint." These renovations have been top to bottom, with properties being brought up to code to provide a decent place to live, rather than slipping back into disrepair and abandonment.

Land banks are also proving to be tools for economic development. From the massive construction of the Amazon fulfillment center in North Randall, Ohio to the redevelopment of an abandoned corner building at 4th and Ashland roads in Mansfield into a Rex's Landscaping center, land banks are proving to be adept at acquiring and repurposing properties in communities large and small. In both of these situations the local county land banks had end users in mind—and repurposed these properties relatively quickly.

But there will be cases where there is no readily apparent path to repurpose a property. It may be so distressed and so contaminated that nobody wants to touch it—under any circumstances. It may appear counterintuitive, but that may be the best time for the land bank to acquire that property. Why? Because while it may take years to develop a strategy to clean the property and repurpose it, much of the work to advance the property cannot be done until the property has been foreclosed and is in "friendly hands." And, with immunity being granted to county land banks in Ohio under S.B. 353 for holding contaminated property, there is some protection to land banks that take a risk on these properties.

The full extent of land bank powers has not yet been fully realized. As land banks continue to evolve they will take on yet-to-be-determined challenges. What is known for certain is that the county land bank has become an indispensable tool in dealing with the challenges of tax delinquent and vacant property in Ohio. These challenges go to all communities, large and small—and beyond to other states throughout the country.

In 2018, county land banks in Ohio incorporated as the Ohio County Land Bank Association. The goal of this organization is to continue the good work of land banks by advocating for resources for additional blight removal of residential and commercial properties, working to refine and improve the original land bank bill, S.B. 353, and above all to share best practices between Ohio counties. The group meets quarterly to hear from members and from experts in the field of redevelopment, blight removal, greening of vacant properties, environmental remediation, and any other topics that might be relevant to the work they are doing. Most importantly, they hear from each other, sharing their problems and potential solutions. They have come to realize that any solutions to their problems must be arrived at through collective action—and through this action, there is hope.

Appendix A

County	Moving Ohio Forward			Neighborhood Initiative Program		Combined Programs	
Source of funds	Ohio Attorney General (robo-signing settlement)			US Treasury - TARP funds			
Eligibility	All Ohio Counties			Ohio County Land Banks only			
	Allocation	Local Match (Over $500,000)	Structures Demolished	Current Allocation	Structures Demolished through 2019	Total Demolition Funds	Structures razed through 2019
Adams	$ 137,507		23	$ 81,373	6	$ 218,880	29
Allen	$ 691,647	$ 191,647	135	$ 3,609,455	219	$ 4,492,749	354
Ashland	$ 282,361		33		5	$ 282,361	38
Ashtabula	$ 533,716	$ 33,716	48	$ 4,350,769	235	$ 4,918,201	283
Athens	$ 158,998		18		15	$ 158,998	33
Auglaize	$ 233,464		23	$ -		$ 233,464	23
Belmont	$ 225,102		22	$ 446,701	31	$ 671,803	53
Brown	$ 356,239		49	$ -		$ 356,239	49
Butler	$ 2,814,690	$ 2,314,690	511	$ 3,695,557	275	$ 8,824,937	786
Carroll	$ 149,815		19			$ 149,815	19
Champaign	$ 266,283		32			$ 266,283	32
Clark	$ 989,535	$ 489,535	186	$ 2,153,627	131	$ 3,632,697	317
Clermont	$ 700,735	$ 200,735	69			$ 901,470	69
Clinton	$ 312,995		38	$ 750,000	34	$ 1,062,995	72
Columbiana	$ 557,823	$ 57,823	72	$ 2,832,241	162	$ 3,447,887	234
Coshocton	$ 214,171		23			$ 214,171	23
Crawford	$ 297,634		40	$ 1,293,750	73	$ 1,591,384	113
Cuyahoga*	$ 12,904,931	$ 12,404,931	3,449	$ 63,116,055	4519	$ 88,425,917	7,968
Darke	$ 255,955		20			$ 255,955	20
Defiance	$ 196,989		20			$ 196,989	20
Delaware	$ 542,233	$ 42,233	37			$ 584,466	37
Erie	$ 495,434		47	$ 965,308	57	$ 1,460,742	104
Fairfield	$ 612,771	$ 112,771	47	$ 995,966	43	$ 1,721,508	90
Fayette	$ 204,370		19		4	$ 204,370	23
Franklin	$ 8,619,466	$ 8,119,466	1,800	$ 23,114,879	999	$ 39,853,811	2,799
Fulton	$ 227,493		15			$ 227,493	15
Galia	$ 96,800		17			$ 96,800	17
Geauga	$ 452,874		33			$ 452,874	33
Greene	$ 652,305	$ 152,305	118			$ 804,610	118
Guernsey	$ 201,578		28	$ 190,791	12	$ 392,369	40
Hamilton	$ 6,357,205	$ 5,857,205	1,626	$ 10,548,948	497	$ 22,763,358	2,123
Hancock	$ 425,267		54			$ 425,267	54
Hardin	$ 175,670		17			$ 175,670	17
Harrison	$ 84,010		7			$ 84,010	7
Henry	$ 150,962		17	$ 54,866	5	$ 205,828	22
Highland	$ 316,850		41	$ -		$ 316,850	41
Hocking	$ 165,575		18			$ 165,575	18
Holmes	$ 114,588		17			$ 114,588	17
Huron	$ 354,538		27			$ 354,538	27
Jackson	$ 185,627		22	$ 90,392	9	$ 276,019	31
Jefferson	$ 308,177		26	$ 2,962,897	187	$ 3,271,074	213
Knox	$ 423,400		48			$ 423,400	48
Lake	$ 812,431	$ 312,431	59	$ 1,250,000	48	$ 2,374,862	107
Lawrence	$ 241,826		45	$ 3,518,464	207	$ 3,760,290	252
Licking	$ 934,446	$ 434,446	139	$ 1,068,627	61	$ 2,437,519	200
Logan	$ 308,436		46	$ 79,267	6	$ 387,703	52
Lorain	$ 2,265,410	$ 1,765,410	229	$ 5,460,246	229	$ 9,491,066	458
Lucas	$ 3,860,507	$ 3,360,507	1,008	$ 29,001,458	2118	$ 36,222,472	3,126
Madison	$ 190,903		16			$ 190,903	16
Mahoning	$ 1,608,184	$ 1,108,184	308	$ 14,814,254	1087	$ 17,530,622	1,395
Marion	$ 498,866		75	$ 850,000	54	$ 1,348,866	129
Medina	$ 581,466	$ 81,466	35			$ 662,932	35
Meigs	$ 79,169		8			$ 79,169	8

County	Moving Ohio Forward			Neighborhood Initiative Program		Combined Programs	
Source of funds	Ohio Attorney General (robo-signing settlement)			US Treasury - TARP funds			
Eligibility	All Ohio Counties			Ohio County Land Banks only			
County	Allocation	Local Match (Over $500,000)	Structures Demolished	Current Allocation	Structures Demolished through 2019	Total Demolition Funds	Structures razed through 2019
Mercer	$ 145,335		16			$ 145,335	16
Miami	$ 576,790	$ 76,790	55			$ 653,580	55
Monroe	$ 38,196		3			$ 38,196	3
Montgomery	$ 4,390,088	$ 3,890,088	938	$ 18,047,139	1162	$ 26,327,315	2,100
Morgan	$ 68,199		11			$ 68,199	11
Morrow	$ 236,063		21			$ 236,063	21
Muskingum	$ 466,590		43	$ -		$ 466,590	43
Noble	$ 71,158		8			$ 71,158	8
Ottawa	$ 240,796		27	$ 441,226	20	$ 682,022	47
Paulding	$ 120,196		13	$ 216,387	22	$ 336,583	35
Perry	$ 217,153		23	$ 393,750	14	$ 610,903	37
Pickway	$ 300,477		49			$ 300,477	49
Pike	$ 109,066		14			$ 109,066	14
Portage	$ 883,666	$ 383,666	129	$ 957,429	68	$ 2,224,761	197
Preble	$ 358,231		35			$ 358,231	35
Putnam	$ 106,130		14			$ 106,130	14
Richland	$ 805,993	$ 305,993	121	$ 3,914,735	330	$ 5,026,721	451
Ross	$ 402,059		36	$ 350,000	13	$ 752,059	49
Sandusky	$ 311,211		25	$ 450,000	20	$ 761,211	45
Scioto	$ 317,672		37	$ 1,999,448	103	$ 2,317,120	140
Seneca	$ 307,652		30	$ 750,000	40	$ 1,057,652	70
Shelby	$ 275,127		23	$ 1,035,141	66	$ 1,310,268	89
Stark	$ 2,461,474	$ 1,961,474	492	$ 12,032,446	768	$ 16,455,394	1,260
Summit	$ 3,971,632	$ 3,471,632	872	$ 9,551,271	634	$ 16,994,535	1,506
Trumbull	$ 1,388,088	$ 888,088	374	$ 13,448,477	739	$ 15,724,653	1,113
Tuscarawas	$ 389,704		32			$ 389,704	32
Union	$ 305,285		20	$ -		$ 305,285	20
Van Wert	$ 172,486		19	$ 1,650,000	55	$ 1,822,486	74
Vinton	$ 62,011		16			$ 62,011	16
Warren	$ 500,000		47			$ 500,000	47
Washington	$ 161,542		19			$ 161,542	19
Wayne	$ 470,538		50			$ 470,538	50
Williams	$ 205,092		19	$ 432,508	22	$ 637,600	41
Wood	$ 633,689	$ 133,689	86			$ 767,378	86
Wyandot	$ 108,401		12			$ 108,401	12
						$ -	-
TOTAL	$ 76,407,217	$ 48,150,921	14,608	$ 242,965,847	15,404	$ 367,523,985	30,012

*NOTE: In addition to the above programs, Cuyahoga County was allocated $50 million in local funds.

The City of Cleveland provided an additional $85.6 million for demolition since 2006.

	$ 50,000,000	3300 est.
	$ 85,600,000	5700 est.
Grand Total	$ 503,123,985	39,012

125

Appendix B

If Dorothy could click her heals and get a Land Bank Authority, what might it look like.......

........A Land Bank on Steroids!!!

To: James Rokakis,
County Treasurer
Land Bank Steering Committee
From: Gus Frangos, Staff
Date: 11-13-07
Re: Ideas and Visions for a County Land Bank

I. Introduction

A publicly created or authorized "county land bank authority" addressing the needs for strategic land planning and land reclamation is urgently needed in Cuyahoga County. Any policy initiative exists in a context. Our context nationally, statewide, County and inner-citywide (unfortunately, on a paralyzing level) consists of a foreclosure crisis (tax and private) which adds to an already decades-old crisis of land abandonment and decay. The model afforded by the Genesee County, Michigan Land Bank serves as a basis for modeling such a Land Bank in Cuyahoga County, Ohio

To date, we chisel away at the causes and the symptoms of the foregoing crisis. In the end, these efforts, if we are honest, are feeble compared to the scope of the problem. In addition to this overwhelming scope, the sporadic and politically dispersed efforts at combating the problems often work at cross-purposes with those advocates seeking a more strategic and unified effort. Community Development organizations have advocated for such a more unified and broad based approach to addressing the problem and information gathering by pointing to the Genesee County, Michigan model.

To this end, the Cuyahoga County Treasurer James Rokakis has proposed a policy initiative that seeks to seriously evaluate the Genesee County model in particular, and a County Land Bank Authority generally, which would allow a more strategic and comprehensive approach to land reclamation and reutilization generally, and combating the problem of vacant and abandoned property specifically.

The Genesee model emanates from a fundamentally different State Constitutional construct. Individual taxing districts are responsible for collecting their taxes. If the taxes become delinquent, the Treasurer then becomes involved in collection. In general, foreclosed and non-bidded, bundled auctioned properties end up in the land bank The reverse is the case in Ohio. Constitutionally, Treasurers are charged with collecting taxes, then distributing them to the various political subdivisions, and finally serving as the enforcer of tax delinquency through the Treasurer's attorney, the County Prosecutor. Though, many laws must be modified and new ones enacted to create or enable the County Land Bank Authorities, Treasurer Rokakis seeks consensus on the concepts and ideas predicate to fashioning such laws, and then advance these concepts and ideas into concrete legislation.

To fashion such consensus, it is useful to throw into a basket the "wish list" of things that administrators, community development officials, neighborhood groups and activists, lenders, lawyers, political officials, etc. have, for years advocated (or struggled with) in dealing with the task of effective land reclamation. The hope is to assemble into this basket the collective wisdom of these "stakeholders" so as to eventually achieve a **consensus of ideas** from which to construct County Land Bank Authorities in Ohio.

Using the Genesee model and its functionality as our inspiration, below is an initial stab at what a County Land Bank Authority might look like. Without considerations (at least for now) of legislative changes, funding sources, etc.... *What if...*

II. What If...

A. Intake and Advanced Assessment

This Land Bank ("LB") would be able to acquire properties through direct purchase, gifts from individuals or cities, tax foreclosure, eminent domain, banks and receivership. Intake assessment would evaluate the land on various levels, i.e. suitability for redevelopment, rehab joint ventures, turning it over to a homeowner, resale, demolition, strategic holding, rental, etc. Assessment would include political considerations and input from appropriate stakeholders. A developed cadre of intake professionals would make the foregoing assessments and evaluate the costs thereof. In addition to physical assessment, lands would be assessed strategically for best results, and greatest impact on distresses communities.

B. Operations

The LB would have an operational component capable of operating internally as well as contractually for outside services. After intake, properties would be demolished as needed, operated, maintained, held or resold for a profit; or rehabbed and sold, or sold to rehabbers. The LB would have broad authority to administer and manage property generally. Short term rehab loans secured by property equity would be available. A precedent exists somewhat in current Ohio law whereby a Treasurer can petition to be appointed a receiver of tax delinquent property and collect the revenues of the property until the taxes are paid.

C. Property Maintenance

Similar to B above, the LB would be equipped with the ability to perform nuisance abatement demolitions, weed cutting, board-ups, etc. on owned and non-owned properties, and, in the case of non-owned properties acquire priority liens on the tax duplicate as is the current practice for city demolition and weed cutting costs. The LB would, of course have a contingent of property maintenance staff or contractors from the maintenance, repair and upkeep of properties during the LB's holding period. perhaps an inventory of supplies such as siding, copper, useable appliances, etc., taken from assessed properties can be maintained for LB use or resale to rehabbers thereby avoiding the vandalism of scavengers. Perhaps a small revenue stream might result from this. Qualified Local Development Corporations would be actively involved in these processes, as well as assessment and planning.

D. Funding and Finance

Legislation would be passed providing for a variety of revenue stream: For example:

1.) Typical city and county-related rehabilitation and nuisance abatement programs;

2.) rental income;

3.) profit from property resales;

4.) perhaps a 1/3 Mill tax;

5.) D-TAC Funds generally, increased however to 10% per tax foreclosure (from the current 5%)

6.) TIFF funding on select projects or targeted areas;

7.) limited and capped general bonding authority piggy-backing onto the state's or county's full faith and credit;

8.) typical municipal and county community development low interest brownfield or development loans;

9.) "tax anticipation" debt instruments transferred to the LB whereby banks would lend based on anticipated tax delinquency receipts, but at lower rates of interest than the loan. The LB would in turn charge a higher rate of penalty and interest (much like a tax lien certificate holder) making the loan arbitrage spread better by being backed by the County's full faith and credit,   or even better, by the State's full faith and credit (so long as it remains locally controlled, however).

10.) Alternatively to the debt instruments, the LB could also function much like a tax lien certificate holder but perhaps enhanced with the county's full faith and credit in order to get better interest rates to help pay as close to par value as possible for the tax lien certificates.

11.) Cooperatives with lenders to charge administrative charges for assessment services, board up, and other sundry services, and loan counseling and foreclosure prevention counseling to first-time borrowers or borrowers in distress;

12.) An excise of $5.00 (or some amount) on conveyances, all building permits issued in the County, foreclosure filing fees, deeds, earmarked for the LB;

13.) The LB would be able to collect rent, invest funds on a short term basis, make revolving rehab loans (and charge favorable interest)

14.) Etc., etc.,

An accounting department would not only provide government compliance and general accounting services, but would provide ongoing "calibration" of estimated borrowing/debt capacity based on shifting tax anticipation not only county-wide but also on a geographically targeted basis. Joint arrangements with municipalities on a geographic basis could result in "joint venturing" and sharing the profit yield between the LB and municipalities in situations where cities themselves find it useful to be a lender (including their own "lender") at little or no interest in exchange for the payment of anticipated taxes to such cities individually as enhanced by penalties and interest.

E. Property Management
The LB would be able to collect rent, show properties, engage realtors, direct needed property maintenance, pursue sales, rehabilitation and acquisition leads (much like a real estate brokerage), or property disposition. It would serve eviction notices, handle complaints, and pursue evictions either in-house or through contract services. Qualified Local Development Corporations would be actively involved in these processes, as well as assessment and planning.

F. Administration.
The LB would have a full-time clerical, executive, accounting and legal staff. The LB would be run like a business so that its activities could be as self sustaining as possible.

G. Governance
The LB would be self-governed with a Board of directors consisting of 5-18 stakeholders, and an advisory board, but with sufficient controls to prevent unqualified personnel or unbecoming political interference. The goal is a very task/result-oriented board to establish policy but allow broad delegation to execute such policy to the staff.

H. Legal
The legal aspects of this effort would fall into two broad categories

each with several sub-categories. The first would be legislation. The LB would require much legislative authorization and changes, and creating the LB Authority itself with its unique functionalities and funding sources. Essential is to the legislative effort would be to tailor the LB's functionalities so that they either mirror or can piggy-back onto existing agency functionalities. In this way, cities, Treasurers, code enforcers, etc., will hopefully interact with the LB in ways with which they are familiar. This will also promote "buy-in."

A sub-category of legislation would include things that are not necessarily related to creation of the LB, but nevertheless essential to the LB success. For example, legislation authorizing joint agreements with municipalities in code enforcement, nuisance abatement and cross-landbanking would be helpful; legislation eliminating conveyance fees on all LB-related sales, and conveyance fee remittance to the LB on all LB acquisitions; reduced foreclosure filing fees like with tax foreclosures, full access to County data bases; deed recording fee waiver; and of course, the tax exemption of all properties in the LB.

The second broad category of legal work, of course would include title work, purchase and sale contracts, evictions, foreclosure, due diligence (administering procurement of needed Surveys, Phase I's, Structural Assessments, and Appraisals), leasing, code compliance, and government audit and compliance.

I. Code Enforcement Partnerships

This LB would have defined code enforcement authority in areas where it would not be a conflict to do so, i.e. proscribing enforcing on land targeted for acquisition by the LB itself. Demolition and nuisance abatement services can be shared as well. Legislation authorizing joint agreements with municipalities in code enforcement, nuisance abatement and cross-landbanking would promote strategic enforcement where cities are unable to do so due to funding or political constraints.

J. Outreach and Political

The LB would coordinate with community groups and cities to make sure efforts are coordinated and not at cross-purposes. More importantly, this office would help prioritize the strategic acquisition and disposition of properties in and out of the LB.

K. Possible In-House Brokerage, Escrow and Title Services.
It may be that the LB can provide quantities of title reports for the Treasurer's foreclosures, or banks in order to keep costs down and create some revenue; third party escrow services for buyers and sellers or lenders engaged in rehab or redevelopment; brokerage services on the buying end of a transaction (disclosed co-broking). These could be good profit centers or potential distractions to the mission, and at worst could create unintended conflicts, but worth mulling over. Brokerage may be a good thing so as to have complete access to MLS services.

L. Eminent Domain and Receivership

This LB might want limited eminent domain authority and enhanced receivership authority under an improved receivership statute.

M. Foreclosure Prevention Counseling and Services

This LB would provide literature, education and assistance to first-time buyers and borrowers in distress. Borrowers completing a course, for example, could be given a slight reduction in interest. Cooperative agreements with Lenders to provide such benefits could be explored.

III. Conclusion

The foregoing ideas are just that—ideas. Not only would they necessarily involve a massive legislative effort, many may not be at all desirable upon further critical analysis. This memo is designed to foster both critical analysis, further concept/idea memos, and ultimately concrete proposals.

Appendix C

OHIO COUNTY LAND BANKS

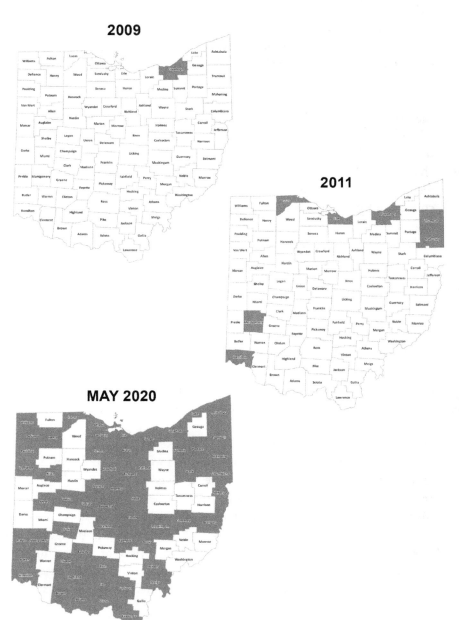

2009

2011

MAY 2020

Notes

Chapter 1:

"the sale of property tax liens"

Real estate taxes are a lien on a property, meaning the charge stays with the property itself rather than the property owner. The county treasurer's job is to collect these taxes and distribute them to the taxing districts (schools, municipalities, libraries, etc.). When the current year's property taxes are unpaid they are considered delinquent and the tax lien may be sold to an investor. The investor pays the amount of the tax lien (perhaps at a discount or premium) and takes over the responsibility of collection of the delinquent tax amounts, often charging high interest rates. The taxing district benefits because they receive their tax revenue in a lump sum rather than having to wait for collection by the treasurer. The investor benefits from a high interest rate. The property owner loses as they now face a less friendly tax collector, a high interest rate and the threat of a quick foreclosure.

"linked deposit program"

A linked deposit involves the relationship between the interest earned on funds deposited at a bank and the loans offered by that bank. In this case, the county treasurer purchased certificates of deposit (CDs) with a participating bank at an interest rate 3 percentage points below the going interest rate. In turn, the bank made loans to homeowners at a rate 3 percentage points below the current loan interest rate. In this way, the bank deposit is linked with the loans made by the bank.

"Housing Court Judge Ray Pianka"

The Cleveland Municipal Housing Court is a special purpose court created in 1979 by the Ohio legislature. It diverted all housing, building and environmental cases from the general docket of the Cleveland Municipal Court to the Housing Court. This was done to allow the judge to develop a special expertise in the area of building and housing, but also to keep these cases out of a revolving docket that prevented continuity and expertise from being developed by the court on individual cases. Today it is the busiest municipal court in the state and employs a staff of over 50 people.

"property tax foreclosures, which I followed, but mortgage foreclosures"
A property tax foreclosure is initiated by the county treasurer for failure to pay property taxes during two current tax cycles. Once taxes have fallen delinquent, a foreclosure usually is filed within a year, sometime longer. A taxpayer may enter into a payment plan to avoid tax foreclosure. A mortgage foreclosure is initiated by a bank for failure to make a mortgage payment. Typically banks will file foreclosures after three months of missed payments.

"yield spread premiums"
A yield spread premium (YSP) is the **fee paid to a mortgage broker** by a wholesale lender for bringing in a loan at a higher interest rate than the going rate. It is a reward to the broker for the higher yielding loan that makes more money over the course of the loan for the lender.

"one of twelve Federal Reserve Bank regional offices in the country"
The Federal Reserve is the central bank of the United States. Its main duties are to supervise and regulate banks, set national monetary policy, provide banking service, promote consumer protection and community development, and maintain financial stability.

"the Home Mortgage Disclosure Act (HMDA), the Home Ownership and Equity Protection Act (HOEPA)"
The Home Mortgage Disclosure Act (Public Law No. 94-200, 89 Stat. 1124) was enacted by Congress in 1975 and requires financial institutions to keep publicly available records of mortgage lending data. The Home Ownership and Equity Protection Act (Public Law No. 103-325, 108 Stat. 2190), originally enacted in 1994, seeks to protect consumers from equity-stripping, high-cost mortgages.

Chapter 3
"no ultimate authority to accelerate the foreclosure actions."
The treasurer is essentially the tax collector and "client;" the prosecutor is the treasurer's "attorney;" and the court is the adjudicator of the proceeding.

"six separate governmental bodies, each of them elected by the public"
This was before the 2010 Cuyahoga County Charter Amendment

established an executive form of county government that eliminated four of the six offices as elective.

"enter it onto the clerk's docket."
Once the decree is journalized, it is entered into a docket which is a record of everything that occurred in the proceeding and is publicly available on the Clerk of Courts Website. https://cpdocket.cp.cuyahogacounty.us/tos.aspx

"The order of the sale contained the legal description of the property"
Historically, there was uncertainty about whether only Clerks of Court could issue orders of sale. HB 138 clarified that, confirming that judicial decrees themselves could contain the order to the sheriff to sell the property following a tax foreclosure decree. See: R.C. 2327.02

"bankruptcy stays, lis pendens"
In the context of delaying the filing of a tax foreclosure on a property, this means that there is already an active proceeding against the property, such as another private mortgage foreclosure. In the context of lien recognition, a foreclosure will eliminate all subordinate liens after a completed tax foreclosure for all those liens that were of record and named as defendants in the case. For lien holders filing their liens after a case is filed, their lien will not attach to the property, though they may retain a money claim against the party who owes a debt to the lienholder.

"examples where tax foreclosures and tax enforcement occurred, at least initially, at an administrative level"
See e.g. https://www.justia.com/foreclosure/judicial-vs-non-judicial-foreclosure/ and https://www.auction.com/blog/judicial-vs-non-judicial-foreclosures/. There was very little precisely on administrative tax foreclosure, but my research showed that states like Missouri and Georgia had proceedings which I sensed were similar. But there was much literature on non-judicial foreclosures generally, which a browser inquiry would reveal. This suggested that the forum of a foreclosure, per se, was not something reserved in any holy grail to courts.

"Chapters 5721 and 323 of the Ohio Revised Code"
Ohio Revised Code 323.25 and 5721.18. The Ohio Rules of Civil Procedure, Rule 1 recognized that certain classes of proceedings were "statutory" and did not require application of the civil rules.

"tax foreclosure is obviously a creature of statute."
In other words, tax foreclosure is not a common law legal concept guided by courts and court precedent. Taxes can only be collected if there are statutes prescribing the nature and reason of the taxes. Enforcement of these taxes arise outside of the common law through the procedures prescribed by the legislature.

"be routed to the new administrative body rather than a judge"
When any case including tax foreclosures gets filed it is randomly assigned to one of the Cuyahoga Common Pleas judges.

"board of revision"
The board of revision (BOR) is a statutory board composed of three elected officials: the county auditor, county treasurer and one county commissioner. While each county has a board of revision, in some larger counties the three elected officials serving on the board will appoint representatives to serve. The primary function of the BOR is to hear complaints regarding property values from property owners. The board holds hearings and makes value decisions which may be appealed to either the Court of Common Pleas or the Board of Tax Appeals. With the passage of HB 294 the BOR may decide foreclosure cases on vacant and abandoned properties.

"(later reduced to twenty-eight days)"
The reduction from 45 days to 28 days occurred in the revisions to SB 172. See: https://legiscan.com/OH/text/SB172/2013

"no one is obligated to maintain or pay taxes on the property"
In cases where a difficult land assembly is occurring over a period of years and a particular property may require environmental remediation, it may be advantageous to allow the property to stay in forfeiture until the remediation or development is ripe for development. An example might be the lengthy work done in Cleveland's "Opportunity Zone."

"approximately thirty-four cases"
The 34 cases were the equivalent of our dry run. Other than a few logistics with file retention and delivery back and forth between the treasurer's office and the clerk of court's office, the process went smoothly.

"In anticipation of a robust use of the new H.B. 294 process [...] to be used by other counties electing to invoke BOR tax foreclosures"
This compendium may be accessed as the "playbook" for land banks and is available on the website of Western Reserve Land Conservancy. https://www.wrlandconservancy.org/county-land-banks/playbook_home/

"An additional fifteen counties use HB 294"
This number represents the results of a survey sent to all Ohio county land banks. Delaware, Morrow, and Seneca counties did not respond.

Chapter 5:
"summarized the input of the working group'
See Appendix B: Dorothy memo

"result in the capture and setting apart of the tax penalty and interest"
From the onset of our efforts, we knew that a dedicated funding stream for operations would not be forthcoming from the state, county or localities. They were all squeezed by the financial crisis. Hence we had to try and find a way of arbitraging the use of existing flows or real estate tax dollars in a way that did not encroach up the tax corpus payable to taxing districts from the real estate tax collections.

"the amendments as written"
A complete review of the highlighted changes can be viewed on the Ohio Senate website by going to the Senate bills passed in the 127th General Assembly, specifically SB 353. http://archives.legislature.state.oh.us/search.cfm
See also: Ohio Revised Code 307.781; 319.43; 321.341; 321.36

"taxing districts"
There are 101 taxing districts in Cuyahoga County.

Chapter 6:
"collectively received tens of millions of dollars to remove vacant and abandoned homes in their counties."
See Appendix A for county-by-county breakdown of funding allocations and demolitions.

Citations

Chapter 1
"at the cost to county taxpayers of $114 million"
"Ohio Treasurer Indicted for Investments." *Washington Post*, June 24,
1995. https://www.washingtonpost.com/archive/politics/1995/06/24/
ohio-treasurer-indicted-for-investments/0f73eb80-7601-4cf5-9bb3-
797af224fa19/

"County Treasurer Convicted in Investment Fund's $115
Million Loss." *AP News*, December 18, 1995. https://apnews.
com/08edd41740cea0e9b8cf50a5ca6e4753

Pierog, Karen. "Cuyahoga Treasurer Accepts Blame, Cites Factors behind
Fund's Demise." *American Banker*, November 22, 1994. https://www.
americanbanker.com/news/cuyahoga-treasurer-accepts-blame-cites-
factors-behind-funds-demise

"much of that money was recovered through litigation"
Norris, Floyd. "Orange County's Bankruptcy: The Overview; Orange
County Crisis Jolts Bond Market." *The New York Times*, December 8,
1994. https://www.nytimes.com/1994/12/08/business/orange-county-s-
bankruptcy-the-overview-orange-county-crisis-jolts-bond-market.html

"dollars that had been perceived as uncollectible."
Johnston, Laura. "New Plan for Selling Tax Liens in Cuyahoga County
Is Making Supporters of Skeptics." cleveland.com, October 25, 2011.
https://www.cleveland.com/cuyahoga-county/2011/10/new_plan_for_
selling_tax_liens_in_cuyahoga_county_is_making_supporters_of_
skeptics.html

"nearly a million dollars in linked deposit loans each month."
Nieves, Felipe. "Cuyahoga County's Subsidized Home Enhancement
Loan Program Invests $103 Million over 10 Years." cleveland.com,
August 13, 2009. https://www.cleveland.com/metro/2009/08/cuyahoga_
countys_subsidized_ho.html

"the Housing Enhancement Loan Program (HELP), is still available today."
"Housing Enhancement Loan Program (HELP)." Accessed June 20, 2019. https://cuyahogacounty.us/development/residents/home-repair-and-remodeling/housing-enhancement-loan-program.

"the lending model depicted by George Bailey and the movie It's a Wonderful Life*"*
It's a Wonderful Life. Directed by Frank Capra. Performed by James Stewart. Liberty Films, 1946.

"Both professors had been studying and writing about subprime loans [...] and securitization"
Engel, Kathleen C., and Patricia A. McCoy, The CRA Implications of Predatory Lending (2002). *Fordham Urban Law Journal,* Vol. 29, 2002, p. 1571. http://dx.doi.org/10.2139/ssrn.315103

Engel, Kathleen C., and Patricia A. McCoy. "Predatory Lending: What Does Wall Street Have to Do with It?" *Housing Policy Debate,* Vol. 15, no. 3, 2004, p. 715. https://doi.org/10.1080/10511482.2004.9521518.

Engel, Kathleen C., and Patricia A. McCoy. "Turning a Blind Eye: Wall Street Finance of Predatory Lending." *Fordham Law Review,* Vol. 75, no. 4, 2007, p. 2039. https://ir.lawnet.fordham.edu/cgi/viewcontent.cgi?article=4248&context=flr

"achieved the goal of home ownership"
Zandi, Mark M. *Financial Shock: A 360 Look at the Subprime Mortgage Implosion, and How to Avoid the Next Financial Crisis.* FT Press, 2008, p. 47-48.

"bundling of mortgages and selling them as bonds"
Muolo, Paul, and Mathew Padilla. *Chain of Blame: How Wall Street Caused the Mortgage and Credit Crisis.* John Wiley & Sons, Inc., 2008, p. 207-208.

"from 16,000 to 263,000 mortgages between 1993 and 1999"
Gramlich, Edward M. "Tackling Predatory Lending: Regulation and Education." Cleveland State University, Cleveland, Ohio. March 23, 2001. https://www.federalreserve.gov/boarddocs/speeches/2001/20010323/default.htm

"nearly 22 percent of the residential loan market"
Muolo and Padilla, p. 185.

"Exploding ARMs"
Center for Responsible Lending. "Subprime 'Exploding' ARMs Pose High Risks for Debt-Strapped Families." September 20, 2006. https://www.responsiblelending.org/media/subprime-exploding-arms-pose-high-risks-debt-strapped-families

"'Liar's loans', or NINJA loans"
Kagan, Julia. "NINJA Loan Definition." *Investopedia,* Updated February 21, 2020. https://www.investopedia.com/terms/n/ninja-loan.asp

"Implode-O-Meter"
"The Mortgage Lender Implode-O-Meter." Accessed June 20, 2019. https://ml-implode.com/

"Slavic Village, ZIP code 44105, was the center of the mortgage foreclosure crisis"
Kotlowitz, Alex. "All Boarded Up." *The New York Times Magazine,* March 8, 2009.

"highest in the country"
Simon, Scott. "In Cleveland, Foreclosures Decimate Neighborhoods." *NPR,* May 24, 2008. https://www.npr.org/templates/story/story.php?storyId=90745303

"twice what it was in 1995"
Schiller, Zach and April Hirsch. "Foreclosure Growth in Ohio 2008." *Policy Matters Ohio,* April, 2008. http://www.policymattersohio.org/wp-content/uploads/2011/10/ForeclosureGrowthInOhio2008.pdf

"Subprime Mortgages: America's Latest Boom and Bust"
Gramlich, Edward M. *Subprime Mortgages: America's Latest Boom and Bust.* The Urban Institute Press, 2007.

"his 1996 speech about tech stocks and the tech market"
Greenspan, Alan. "The Challenge of Central Banking in a Democratic Society." The American Enterprise Institute for Public Policy Research, Washington, D.C. December 5, 1996. https://www.federalreserve.gov/BOARDDOCS/SPEECHES/19961205.htm

"in a speech he gave in 2004"
Greenspan, Alan. "Understanding Household Debt Obligations." Credit Union National Association 2004 Governmental Affairs Conference, Washington, D.C. February 23, 2004. https://www.federalreserve.gov/boarddocs/speeches/2004/20040223/

Chapter 2
"Foreclosures in Cuyahoga County went from 5,900 in 2000 to almost 7,000 in 2001"
"Cuyahoga County Foreclosure Filings 1995-2008." *Policy Matters Ohio,* October 25, 2011. http://policymattersohio.org/research-policy/pathways-out-of-poverty/consumer-protection-asset-building/housing-foreclosures/cuyahoga-county-foreclosure-filings-1995-2008

"Ohio's foreclosure rate was triple the national average by 2005."
Katz, Alyssa. *Out Lot: How Real Estate Came to Own Us.* Bloomsbury Publishing, 2009, p. 87.

"That year, 1.4% of all Ohio households were in foreclosure."
Schiller, Zach. "Foreclosure Growth in Ohio 2006." *Policy Matters Ohio,* 2006. http://www.policymattersohio.org/wp-content/uploads/2011/09/foreclosure_growth_ohio_2006.pdf.

"Dayton was first in 2001"
Dayton, Ohio, Ohio Revised Code General Ordinance § 112.43(A) (2001), invalidated by City of Dayton v. Ohio, 813 N.E.2d 707 (Ohio Ct. App. 2004).

"Cleveland and Toledo followed in 2002"
Cleveland, Ohio, Codified Ordinances § 659 (2002).
Toledo, Ohio, Municipal Code §§ 795.21- .23 (2002).

"the Dayton ordinance was preempted by state law"
City of Dayton v. State. 813 N.E.2d 707 (Ohio Ct. App. 2004).

"by 2006, all three cases were decided in favor of the banks"
American Financial Services Ass'n v. City of Cleveland (2006).
American Financial Services Ass'n v. City of Toledo (2006).

"In 2003 we experienced nearly 8,700 foreclosures in Cuyahoga County. In 2004 the number climbed to over 9,700."
Schiller, Zach and Jeremy Iskin. "Foreclosure Growth in Ohio: A Brief Update." *Policy Matters Ohio,* June 2005. https://www.policymattersohio.org/files/research/foreclosuregrowthohio2005.pdf

"owned by Roland Arnall [...] President Bush's pick to become ambassador to the Netherlands."
Muolo, Paul, and Mathew Padilla. *Chain of Blame: How Wall Street Caused the Mortgage and Credit Crisis.* John Wiley & Sons, Inc., 2008, p. 96.

"agreed in 2005 to pay states over $300 million to settle claims against it"
Katz, p. 90-91, 93.

"closing of 229 retail branches and laid off 3,800 employees"
Kristoff, Kathy. M, and David Streitfeld. "Ameriquest Plans to Cut 3,800 Jobs." *Los Angeles Times,* May 3, 2006. https://www.latimes.com/archives/la-xpm-2006-may-03-fi-ameriquest3-story.html.

"over 45,000 loans between 2002 and 2004."
Katz, p. 91.

"By 2005, the city had over 200 vacant properties."
Katz, p. 90.

"Mark Wiseman as its first director"
Weinstein, Alan C., Kathryn W. Hexter, and Molly Schnoke. "Responding to Foreclosures in Cuyahoga County: An Assessment of Progress." *Cleveland State University*, 2006. https://engagedscholarship.csuohio.edu/cgi/viewcontent.cgi?article=1006&context=lawfac_reports.

Chapter 3
"the Rules of Civil Procedure"
(Ohio) https://www.supremecourt.ohio.gov/LegalResources/Rules/civil/CivilProcedure.pdf
(Federal) https://www.federalrulesofcivilprocedure.org/frcp/

"send the order from the court (the judge) to the clerk of courts to journalize"
Ohio Civ. R. 58

"it had to prepare an 'order of sale' "
Ohio Revised Code, 2327.01 et seq

"in a publication of daily circulation"
Ohio Revised Code 5721.19 and 5721.191

"the seminal cases dealing with foreclosure"
Mullane v. Central Bank & Trust Co (1950) 339 U.S. 306; Mennonite
Rd. Bd. of Missions v. Adams (1983) 462 U.S. 791 (1983); Central Trust
v. Jensen (1993) 67 Ohio St. 3d 140.

*"Civil Rule 4 of the Ohio Rules of Civil Procedure applicable to all lawsuits
generally"*
See "the Rules of Civil Procedure" above

"Board of Revision"
Ohio Revised Code Chapter 5715.01 et seq.

*"identified as best suited to hear foreclosure cases on vacant and abandoned
properties."*
Ohio Revised Code 323.66(A)

"pushed for tax lien sales in 1999"
Ohio Revised Code 5721.30 through 5721.40

"we passed the bill by a 90-9 vote on May 10, 2006"
Ohio Legislative Service Commission. "General Assembly 126 (2005-
2006): Final Status Report of Legislation." May 4, 2007. https://www.lsc.
ohio.gov/documents/reference/archives/statusreports/status126/srl126.pdf
HB 294: http://archives.legislature.state.oh.us/fiscalnotes.cfm?ID=126_
HB_294&ACT=As%20Enrolled

"This tracked pre-existing land bank statutes, albeit much more quickly"
Ohio Revised Code 5722.03

"directly transfer tax foreclosed abandoned properties to municipal land banks without exposure to sale"
Ohio Revised Code 323.71

"the auditor's value was rebuttably presumed to be the value of the property"
Ohio Revised Code 323.71 and Ohio Revised Code 373(G)

"if the rebuttable presumption [...] or seek other relief."
Ohio Revised Code 323.71

"amendments to H.B. 294 [...] without reference to auditor's value"
Ohio Revised Code 323.78

"The property then had to be exposed to sale
Ohio Revised Code 5721.19(C)(2)(a)

"all the taxes paid by the new buyer"
Ohio Revised Code 5721.19(D)(3)

"Unlike private mortgage foreclosures"
Ohio Revised Code 2329.20

"minimum bid in tax foreclosure cases is always the taxes, assessments, penalties, and interest"
Ohio Revised Code 5721.19(D)

"this right of a property owner"
Ohio Revised Code 5721.25

"Under the old system [...] deem the municipality to be the purchaser of the property"
Ohio Revised Code 5721.03(D)

"included on the auditor's List of Forfeited Properties"
Ohio Revised Code Chapter 5723.01 et seq.

"alternative right of redemption"
Ohio Revised Code 323.65(J); 323.78

"having the same legal effect of a 'confirmation.'"
Ohio Revised Code 323.76

"Invoking the ARR was in the discretion of the treasurers throughout the state."
Ohio Revised Code 323.78

"In counties that elected not to [...] a conventional sheriff's sale"
Ohio Revised Code 5721.19(C)

"'forfeit' to the State of Ohio"
Ohio Revised Code 5723.01 et seq.

"through periodic auditor's sales"
Ohio Revised Code 5723.06(1) and (2)

"For the first time in Ohio [...] might remain sometimes for decades."
See e.g. Ohio Revised Code 5722.13

"This was later modified in 2014"
Ohio Revised Code 323.69(D)(1)(b)

Chapter 4

"Foreclosures reached 13,943 in 2006 and increased to 14,946 in 2007"
Rothstein, David. "Home Insecurity: Foreclosure Growth in Ohio 2010."
Policy Matters Ohio, March, 2010. https://www.policymattersohio.org/
research-policy/pathways-out-of-poverty/consumer-protection-asset-
building/housing-foreclosures/home-insecurity-2010-foreclosure-growth-
in-ohio

"In 2006, over $30 million had gone uncollected"
Community Research Partners and ReBuild Ohio. "$60 Million and
Counting: The Cost of Vacant and Abandoned Properties to Eight
Ohio Cities." *Greater Ohio Policy Center,* 2008, p. 2-20. https://www.
greaterohio.org/publications/2017/6/20/rebuild-ohio

"ever paying property taxes again was only 5 percent!"
Cuyahoga County Treasurer's Office. Internal Study. Fall 2010.

"In Montgomery County [...] experienced in Columbus"
Community Research Partners and ReBuild Ohio. "$60 Million and
Counting: The Cost of Vacant and Abandoned Properties to Eight Ohio
Cities." *Greater Ohio Policy Center*, 2008. https://www.greaterohio.org/
publications/2017/6/20/rebuild-ohio

"he decided to walk away"
Kotlowitz, Alex. "All Boarded Up." *The New York Times Magazine.* March
8, 2009.

"Census figures put Cleveland's population in 2000 at approximately
480,000 people"
"American FactFinder - Results 2000." U.S. Census Bureau, Accessed
July 2, 2019. https://factfinder.census.gov/faces/tableservices/jsf/pages/
productview.xhtml?pid=DEC_00_SF1_P001&prodType=table

"By 2005 the population was less than 415,000"
"American FactFinder - Results 2005." U.S. Census Bureau, Accessed
July 2, 2019. https://factfinder.census.gov/faces/tableservices/jsf/pages/
productview.xhtml?pid=ACS_05_EST_B01003&prodType=table

"The number dropped to 406,000 by 2006"
"American FactFinder - Results 2006." U.S. Census Bureau, Accessed
July 2, 2019. https://factfinder.census.gov/faces/tableservices/jsf/pages/
productview.xhtml?pid=ACS_06_EST_B01003&prodType=table

"an incredibly complex and sophisticated masterpiece [...] and
intergovernmental collaboration"
Alexander, Frank S. *Land Banks and Land Banking.* 2nd ed., Center for
Community Progress, 2015.

Chapter 5
"where the tax impositions exceeded the auditor's tax assessed value"
Ohio Revised Code 323.71

"It is not acceptable [...] out-of-town landlords."
Fonger, Ron. "Flint Mayor Dayne Walling: No Maintenance on Land
Bank Properties 'Is Not Acceptable.'" mlive.com, October 12, 2011.

https://www.mlive.com/news/flint/2011/10/flint_mayor_dayne_walling_no_m.html

"Delinquent Tax and Collection (DTAC) fund"
Ohio Revised Code 321.261

"economic development or industrial development activities"
Ohio Revised Code 1724.01 et seq.

"new category of CIC called county land reutilization corporations"
Ohio Revised Code 1724.01(A)(3)

"a non-profit entity distinct from government but tied to the government creating it"
Op. Atty. Gen 2000-37; See also: State, ex rel Burton v Greater Portsmouth Growth Corp., (1966) 7 Ohio St. 2d 34.

"Its contracts and liabilities [...] accept that responsibility."
Op. Atty. Gen 1991-071

"CICs are private non-profit corporations with public attributes"
Op. Atty. Gen 1979-061

"The public attributes [...] audit by the state"
Ohio Revised Code 1724.11

"At least one Ohio Attorney General opinion"
Op. Atty. Gen 1979-061

"bidding practices of the Trumbull County Land Bank were challenged"
Triple Diamond Trucking and Excavating LLC v. Trumbull County Land Reutilization Corp. 2018-Ohio-5193, 36-50, 155 Ohio appeal not allowed sub nom Triple Diamond Trucking & Excavating v. Trumbull County Land Reutilization Corp., 2019-Ohio1421, 155 Ohio St. 3d 1422, 120 N.E.3d 868.

"appealed to the Ohio Supreme Court, which denied a writ of certiorari"
Diamond Trucking & Excavating v. Trumbull County Land Reutilization Corp., 2019-Ohio1421, 155 Ohio St. 3d 1422, 120 N.E.3d 868

"electing subdivisions"
Ohio Revised Code 1724(A)(9)

"traditional land bank statute"
Ohio Revised Code 5722.01 et seq.

"exclusively governmental bureaus or departments within a political subdivision"
Ohio Revised Code 5722.01 et seq.

"extending these governmental powers to this new category of CICs"
Ohio Revised Code 1724(A)(9)

"hold property tax exempt like a traditional land bank"
Ohio Revised Code 5722.11 and 5709.12(F)

"be governed by an independent board"
Ohio Revised Code 1724.03

"receive properties from tax foreclosure"
Ohio Revised Code 1724.10

"promote the tax base in a highly nimble and transactional manner"
Ohio Revised Code 1724.02 and 1724.08

"conventional tax foreclosure statutes"
Ohio Revised Code 323.25 and 5721.18

"need only be exposed to one sale"
Ohio Revised Code 5721.19 and 5721.191

"without exposure to sale"
See e.g., Ohio Revised Code 323.71

"tax forfeiture statute"
Ohio Revised Code 5723.01 et seq.

"making a written request"
Ohio Revised Code 5723.04

"legally inspected for environmental, code, and safety issues"
Ohio Revised Code 5723.01(A)(4)

"clear of all taxes, assessments, liens, and encumbrances"
Ohio Revised Code 5723.04(B)

"The enhancement to these sections [...] county land banks"
Ohio Revised Code 715.261

"pursue independent money damage lawsuits against the property owner"
Ohio Revised Code 715.261

"'agency' agreement"
Ohio Revised Code 715.261

"immunized county land banks from environmental liability"
Ohio Revised Code 5722.22

"sovereign immunity upon county land banks"
Ohio Revised Code 2744.01(F)

"Such liens were eliminated, effective on the date of a recorded transfer to a land bank"
e.g., Ohio Revised Code: 715.261; 5723.04; 743.04; 6119.06

"The amendments also gave citizens [...] as a matter of law"
e.g., Ohio Revised Code 715.2261(H) and (I)

"intergovernmental transfers between municipal and county land banks"
Ohio Revised Code 5709.12(F)
"The laws were changed [...] the passage date of S.B. 353"
Ohio Revised Code 5709(F)(1)(a)

"a system of 'consent' from taxing districts"
Ohio Revised Code 5722.06; 5722.09; 5722.21

"The amendments eliminated this application for county land banks"
Ohio Revised Code 5722.06; 5722.09; 5722.21

"another change had to do with advisory boards"
Ohio Revised Code 5722.09

Chapter 6
"so the amendment was introduced and passed on the floor."
Murray, Dennis. Interview. Conducted by Jim Rokakis. Cleveland, Ohio, July 29, 2019

"When the Land Conservancy [...] conservation projects we were able to do each year."
Cochran, Rich. Interview. Conducted by Jim Rokakis. Cleveland, Ohio, October 3, 2019

"At the Land Conservancy we believe [...] historic inner cities and first suburbs?"
Cochran, Rich. Interview. Conducted by Jim Rokakis. Cleveland, Ohio, October 3, 2019

"it's nice to look at but it doesn't take me anywhere"
Sammarone, Charles. Meeting with Jim Rokakis. Cleveland, Ohio, September 12, 2011.

"a piece in the Washington Post *about the need to raise demolition dollars"*
Rokakis, Jim. "When the Best Way to Save a Neighborhood Is to Tear It Down." *Washington Post*, February 10, 2012. https://www.washingtonpost.com/opinions/when-the-best-way-to-save-a-neighborhood-is-to-tear-it-down/2012/01/31/gIQABD4M4Q_story.html

"a very powerful piece about the need to find legal settlement dollars"
Morgenson, Gretchen. "In a Bank Settlement, Don't Forget the Bulldozers." *New York Times*, August 16, 2014. https://www.nytimes.com/2014/08/17/business/in-a-bank-settlement-dont-forget-the-bulldozers.html?

"There Goes the Neighborhood"
"There Goes the Neighborhood." *60 Minutes*. CBS News, December 18, 2011.

"who had been illegally foreclosed upon"
Weise, Karen. "About That 25 Billion Robo-Signing Settlement." *Bloomberg*, November 15, 2012. https://www.bloomberg.com/news/articles/2012-11-15/about-that-25-billion-robo-signing-settlement

"You were very influential [...] have an impact on communities."
DeWine, Mike. Interview. Conducted by Jim Rokakis. Columbus, Ohio, July 30, 2019.

"So we took it from there [...] shouldn't shock us."
DeWine, Mike. Interview. Conducted by Jim Rokakis. Columbus, Ohio, July 30, 2019.

"over 14,600 abandoned structures had been removed."
"Moving Ohio Forward: Demolition Grant Program." Ohio Attorney General's Office, February 2015, p. 6. https://www.ohioattorneygeneral.gov/Files/Publications-Files/Publications-for-Consumers/Foreclosure-Publications/Moving-Ohio-Forward-Program-Summary

"Such behavior, [...] without political interference."
Gelinas, Nicole. "The Rise of the Mortgage 'Walkers.'" *Manhattan Institute*, February 8, 2008. https://www.manhattan-institute.org/html/rise-mortgage-walkers-1171.html

"Don and I [...] to think outside the box as well."
Dworkin, David. Phone Interview. Conducted by Jim Rokakis. December 3, 2019.

"Most of the rest of Treasury [...] to demolish homes."
Graves, Don. Interview. Conducted by Jim Rokakis. Cleveland, Ohio, October 7, 2019.
"Estimating the Effect of Demolishing Distressed Structures in Cleveland, Ohio. 2009-2013: Impacts on Real Estate Equity and Mortgage-Foreclosure"
Griswold, Nigel G., Benjamin Calnin, Michael Schramm, Luc Anselin and Paul Boehnlein. "Estimating the Effect of Demolishing Distressed Structures in Cleveland, OH, 2009-2013: Impacts on Real Estate Equity and Mortgage-Foreclosure." *Western Reserve Land Conservancy*, Report Produced by Griswold Consulting Group, 2013. https://www.wrlandconservancy.org/pdf/FinalReportwithExecSummary.pdf

"a 'playbook' that Gus developed for all land banks"
"Land Bank Playbook." Provided by Thriving Communities Institute of
Western Reserve Land Conservancy. https://www.wrlandconservancy.org/
county-land-banks/playbook_home/

"The Cost of Vacancy – Everybody Pays"
"The Cost of Vacancy – Everybody Pays." *Western Reserve Land
Conservancy*, March 1, 2014. https://www.wrlandconservancy.org/
publications-by-type/special-publications/page/2/

Index

Acknowledgments

Jim Rokakis

There are many people I want to acknowledge for making land banks possible, and for doing the follow up work around land banks and raising the resources that have made land banks so impactful. Cuyahoga County Commissioners Peter Lawson Jones, Jimmy Dimora, and Tim Hagan deserve praise for allowing me to devote so much time and effort during my time as Treasurer to the establishment of a county land bank. State Senator Robert Spada deserves our thanks for carrying the land bank bill in its early stages, but in particular we owe a debt of gratitude to Senator Tom Patton (now a state representative) and State Representative Matt Dolan (now a state senator). Without their efforts and their work to convince the Republican majorities in both houses of the Ohio legislature we would never have passed Senate Bill 353. Tom Patton has continued to be our champion, carrying numerous corrective amendments that we needed to continue to make our Ohio land bank bills effective.

First and foremost, we acknowledge the work of Gus Frangos, which we have done elsewhere in the book. His work as he explains it in Chapters Three, Five, and Seven, is his legacy.

We owe a special thanks to Congressman Dan Kildee. He has been a beacon of light throughout the entire foreclosure crisis and its aftermath. He has used his many talents and skills to devise a strategy, the establishment of county land banks, that has taken root all over America. He was extremely helpful to us and served as a constant source of expertise, inspiration and encouragement. We first met Dan when he was the county treasurer in Genesee County, Michigan. Now, he has taken his considerable talents to Washington, D.C. In Cleveland, we owe special thanks to Frank Ford and Kermit Lind, who provided encouragement and early technical support. Frank, in particular, has been a leader in Northeast Ohio with his research, his vision and wisdom.

We also owe thanks to editorial boards all over Ohio that provided critical editorial support as we attempted to pass both House Bill 294 and Senate Bill 353, and in particular to Becky Gaylord, who at the time was with the *Plain Dealer*.

Thanks to the CEO of Western Reserve Land Conservancy, Rich Cochran, for taking on the mission of land banks and blight removal in the state of Ohio. The monies we have raised to deal with the abandoned property crisis would not have been raised without the intervention and political clout of the Land Conservancy. There are so many people who played a critical role in our efforts, but it was Rich's vision and leadership that moved a traditional land conservation organization into the urban space—and the Land Conservancy made an enormous difference there. In particular, I'd like to thank the board members of Western Reserve Land Conservancy who supported this urban work: Larry Bettcher, Tom Chema, Kevin Conner, Keymah Durden, Ruth Eppig, Lyle Ganske, Sam Hartwell, Chris Hess, Jeff Holland, Ruben Holloway, Rick Hyde, Betsy Juliano, Kathy Leavenworth, John Leech, Tom Liebhardt, David Mayo, Laura McKenna, Scott Mueller, Bill Mulligan, Jane Neubauer, Winnie Nordell, Nancy Ruben, Mitchell Schneider, Muffy Sherwin, Jim Spira, Julie Visconsi, Craig White, and Loyal Wilson. Their involvement in blight removal efforts at the state and federal level made all the difference.

Cleveland City Council has been extremely supportive of land bank work, in particular Councilman Tony Brancatelli who represents Slavic Village and the 44105 ZIP code, widely recognized as the epicenter of the foreclosure crisis in America. Tony's vision and efforts in his neighborhood have provided stability to that community, and elevated the Cuyahoga Land Bank—where he has served as chairman for several years—to new levels of achievement. He has been a voice of calm and reason when many others would have panicked and fled.

Additional gratitude is owed to many public officials, including Governor Mike DeWine, who as attorney general allocated $75 million of a national legal mortgage fraud settlement to assist in our efforts, and the creation of the program that came to be known as "Moving Ohio Forward". We also owe much gratitude to Ohio's United States Senators Sherrod Brown and Rob Portman, who played a critical role in moving the Hardest Hit Fund dollars to Ohio, and ultimately seventeen other states for blight removal. Cleveland Cavaliers' owner Dan Gilbert was enormously helpful to us, and used the resources of his company—Quicken Loans—to provide technical and lobbying support on the effort to repurpose Hardest Hit Fund dollars. Their efforts were critical. I also want to thank Cuyahoga County Executive Armond Budish and Cuyahoga County Council President Dan Brady for making good on the commitment to provide $50 million for blight removal from Cuyahoga County's general fund.

Two other people played an important role in the establishment and operation of land banks. Ed Herman, a Cleveland lawyer and a veteran of the Afghan conflict was invaluable to our efforts. His early research and advocacy on the writing of congressional bills as well as his work with Treasury on obtaining Hardest Hit Fund dollars were essential. Robin Darden Thomas served in Cuyahoga County government for twenty-eight years. She wore many hats in the auditor's office and was my chief deputy in the treasurer's office for fourteen years, finally serving as treasurer in 2011. She joined me at Western Reserve Land Conservancy late in 2011, where she assumed the role of land bank program director. Her knowledge of county government and how county offices interface with land banks is unmatched in Ohio. She facilitated the creation of the first land bank in Cuyahoga County and has been the "go to" person in the state of Ohio on not only how to start a land bank but how to operate a land bank once it has been established. People who affectionately refer to her as "The Mother of County Land Banks" in Ohio are not far off in their description. Tragically, Robin passed away a few months prior to the publication of this book. She is missed dearly by all who knew her, but her legacy lives on in the far-reaching impacts of the land banks she helped get off the ground.

Dan McGraw has been especially helpful and played the role of "roving reporter" as he travelled that state reporting on the progress of twelve of the land banks we featured as vignettes in this book (all but Perry County).

Thanks also to Natalia Perkins and Kelly McCarthy, recent graduates of Smith and Oberlin, who helped edit this book and in particular Kelly who has been especially helpful to see this effort through to its completion.

Finally, I want to thank my wife Laurie, who has listened to me patiently for almost twenty years as I railed against foreclosures, Wall Street, vacant properties, plummeting property values, and the like. She has never complained about the many, many nights this work has taken me away from our home—sometimes for days at a time. Her encouragement has meant so much to me and kept me going on days I questioned whether I was making a difference—or just tilting at windmills.

Gus Frangos

Special thanks must immediately be extended to a brilliant lawyer, Robert Rink. He had special expertise in legislative draftsmanship. He collaborated with me on the drafting of many sections of S.B. 353.

Thank you also to South Euclid Mayor Georgine Welo for being our first board chairman following Jim Rokakis' chairmanship. Her leadership and enormous support in the early days helped steady our ship. Our current chairman, Cleveland City Councilman Anthony Brancatelli, is a titan of neighborhood community development. His leadership and knowledge have been indispensable to our success. Past board member Chris Warren, perhaps the most preeminent expert in neighborhood community and economic development, helped navigate the relationship between the City of Cleveland and the Cuyahoga Land Bank. Chris served on our board as Mayor Frank Jackson's appointee.

Other recognitions include attorney James Sassano of Carlisle, McNellie, Rini, Kramer & Ulrich Co., L.P.A. He provided many insightful suggestions for internal changes in the tax foreclosure process. Thank you Jim.

Legislative expertise and community development expertise from lawyers Kermit Lind, Frank Ford, and Congressman Dan Kildee were all consulted in the crafting of S.B. 353. National land banking expert and attorney at Emory Law School Frank Alexander's writings educated me immensely. Special gratitude to Senator Tom Patton, who was our champion in the General Assembly getting S.B. 353 passed. Profound thanks also to my talented executive assistant of ten years, Jacqui Knettel. She is the glue that keeps our staff knitted together. She has been a trusted advisor to me and knows every nook and cranny of our operations.

Lastly, thanks to my wife Christie who is my best cheerleader and critic. She helped keep me focused and patient. Amazingly, many of my drafting ideas came in the middle of the night while in a state of half-sleep. I would wake up and she would make me write down my thoughts. She has participated in the Cuyahoga Land Bank's work by quietly engaging with our many non-profit partners and faith-based institutions because she loves people and is herself a missionary at heart.

About the Authors

 **Jim Rokakis** is Vice President of Western Reserve Land Conservancy and Director of its Thriving Communities program. He is involved in a number of activities, including the establishment of almost 60 county land banks throughout Ohio and working in Columbus and Washington, D.C. to raise funds for Ohio communities to deal with distressed properties.

Rokakis served for 19 years on the Cleveland City Council – the last seven as chairman of the finance committee. In 1997, Rokakis took office as Cuyahoga County Treasurer. Faced with Cuyahoga County's mortgage foreclosure crisis, Rokakis worked with legislators to have introduced and passed House Bill 294, which streamlined the foreclosure process for abandoned properties. Additionally, Rokakis was the driving force behind a bill that allowed for the creation of the Cuyahoga County Land Reutilization Corporation, also known as the Cuyahoga Land Bank.

Former Attorney General, and current Governor Mike DeWine recently stated that Rokakis was the reason behind his decision to allocate 75 million dollars of Ohio's 93 million dollars from the "Robo-signing" settlement for demolition. Rokakis helped to put the Ohio program and its rules into place. He played an integral role in the U.S. Treasury Department's decision to allocate a portion of the Hardest Hit Fund for demolition and in Cuyahoga County's commitment of $50 million dollars for demolition. Working with the Ohio Congressional delegation he led the effort to reallocate an additional 2 billion dollars to the Hardest Hit Funds in December of 2016—with 192 million of those dollars coming to Ohio. To date, Rokakis has raised almost 450 million for the demolition of almost 40,000 blighted structures in Ohio.

He is the recipient of numerous local, state and national awards, including being named "County Leader of the Year" by American City and County Magazine in 2007, and the recipient of the Cleveland Foundation's Wadsworth Award in 2016. In December 2011, Rokakis was featured on the CBS program "60 Minutes", discussing the need to fund demolition in distressed urban areas. He has written for numerous publications including the Washington Post where he wrote the cover story for the Outlook section about the foreclosure crisis and Cleveland's Slavic Village neighborhood.

Rokakis earned his undergraduate degree at Oberlin College and his Juris Doctorate degree from Cleveland-Marshall School of Law.

Gus Frangos was born and raised in Cleveland Ohio. A musician and music major by early training, Gus switched to the law and attended Cleveland Marshall College of Law where he excelled and graduated with high honors in 1982. He joined the law firm of Ulmer & Berne in 1982 and practiced there until he was elected to Cleveland City Council in 1986. Gus represented the 13th Ward, the downtown ward, from 1986 until 1993. Mr. Frangos served as a Cleveland Municipal Court Magistrate from 1993 to 1997. Throughout 1986 until his employment with the Cuyahoga Land Bank in 2009, Mr. Frangos maintained a private practice of law.

In the Fall of 2004, Mr. Frangos was retained by the Cuyahoga County Treasurer to propose and craft policy changes for the expedited administration and disposition of vacant and abandoned tax delinquent properties. This effort resulted in the drafting and ultimate passage of H.B. 294 which authorized administrative tax foreclosure of vacant and abandoned lands in the various county Boards of Revision. He later authored S.B. 353 which is Ohio's county land bank legislation. All of these reforms were designed to promote efficient land disposition of vacant, abandoned and tax delinquent lands in Ohio. These reforms are widely practiced throughout the state of Ohio and serve as examples for several other states. In fact, Frangos is widely recognized as the preeminent drafter of complex land bank legislation in the country and had consulted with dozens of states and communities around the country.

Mr. Frangos is now the President and General Counsel of the Cuyahoga County Land Reutilization Corporation. He also is the President of the Ohio Land Bank Association which is a statewide association of 56 county land banks.

His concentration and areas of specialty include constitutional, real estate, transactional and administrative law.

9 781950 843237